EQUAL SCRUTINY

Privatization and Accountability in Digital Education

PATRICIA BURCH

ANNALEE G. GOOD

HARVARD EDUCATION PRESS

CAMBRIDGE, MASSACHUSETTS

KH

Library of Congress Control Number 2013952617
Paperback ISBN 978-1-61250-684-5
Library Edition ISBN 978-1-61250-685-2

Published by Harvard Education Press,
an imprint of the Harvard Education Publishing Group

Harvard Education Press
8 Story Street
Cambridge, MA 02138

Cover Design: Steven Pisano
Cover Photo: © Gary John Norman/cultura/Corbis

The typefaces used in this book are Fairfield LH and Quarca

9/30/15

To our families
and all the educators in our lives

CONTENTS

PART THREE

Shifting the Current

INTRODUCTION

PRIVATIZATION AND DIGITAL EDUCATION are surging forward in K–12 public education. That private contracting and digital learning are both on the rise is not coincidental given the policy context. Digital schooling sits at the crosscurrent of several reform paradigms, each of which pushes government contracting and schools' use of technology and data forward: standards-based reform, with schools, districts, and states struggling to produce and account for curriculum and assessment aligned with standards; market-based reform, in which parental choice is a lever for program quality and private vendors (both for-profit and not-for-profit) are among the primary producers of information to inform those choices; and the increased influence of mayors' offices and the business community in school management and organization.

When we began to look more closely at the riptides of education technology and education contracting, three things became apparent. First, there is an enormous amount of investment and policy activity around digital education, in particular digital schools, digital instruction, and digital curriculum. Second, there is scattered and limited research to support the claims that digital education will transform teaching for low-income students in K–12 public schools. And third, as a result of the increased investment and activity, schools and other education agencies are contracting more with primarily for-profit vendors at rapid rates—*buying* as opposed to *making*. This crosscurrent of activity is seismic; there is both opportunity and risk here, with huge reverberations for policy and practice in education.

Most people in the commercial and policy-making worlds refer to digital education as a wave of reform that is attracting the quintessential twenty-first-century teacher—one who is dedicated, Apple smart, Google wise, and generally Internet savvy. This is the teacher who, like the image in so many TV advertisements, outperforms others by

1

out-thinking the competition using new technology: developing content that can be accessed by students anytime and anywhere and personalizing learning through computer-generated algorithms that pinpoint exactly where a student needs help and just in time.

This image of energy and effortless integration inside of schools and classrooms is very seductive, as it is the underlying and larger promise of digital education. Yet, as we looked deeper, we found that the implementation of digital education entailed much more work and many more sacrifices, in the form of actual cash from schools as well as the hidden costs borne by teachers, families, and students (e.g., time, transportation, cost of Internet access, reduced attention to other projects or student needs). While we hear everybody talking about how digital education can democratize information inside schools and classrooms—eliminating the middle man, the bureaucracy, and geographic limitations—there is another set of critical questions that demands equal scrutiny. In public contracts for digital education, we need to be asking:

- What drives digital curriculum and its content?
- What drives instruction and the role of teacher in the digital classroom?
- What drives data, and who has access to the data?
- What is the role of the vendor in these dynamics?

Part of ensuring greater transparency and accountability is empowering states, districts, teachers, parents, and students to know who or what drives these critical elements of digital education before signing onto a contract with a vendor. In other words, who creates the curriculum, and based on what? Who (or what) progresses and manages the pace of instruction, adapts instruction to student needs, assesses student learning, decides what data is accessible via technology, and determines who sees the resulting data? These overlapping questions are important because they help us get beyond the loud talk—the need for more accountability, how technology can save our schools—so that we can see what's behind the surge in digital education and what it really means for public education.

Clearly, digital education has enormous potential to transform teaching and learning, but not without risk. This book explores both the possibilities and the dangers in this surge in digital education and privatization through an in-depth analysis of the instructional setting in multiple types of digital education. Based on this analysis, we developed figure I.1 in order to better visualize the characteristics of these settings and to anchor our analyses of the four questions posed above. In addition, the figure is intended to guide conversations around vendors' influence in digital education toward greater quality, equity, and access, as they are central actors in the rising tide of digital education.

FIGURE I.1   Critical decisions toward quality and access in contracting for digital education

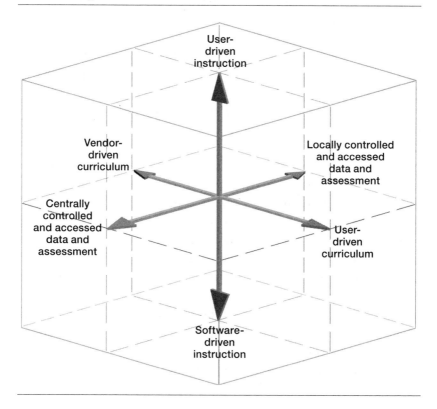

The figure is meant to be conceptual in nature, taking theoretical ideas such as marketization, privatization, and commercialism and bringing them down to size, as they are experienced by educators, students, and parents. It is intended to help districts and others assess who is deciding what in contracts with vendors for digital education. Each of the axes (instruction, curriculum, data, and assessment) is a critical arena whereby vendors influence quality and access in instruction. For example, the extent to which data and assessment are locally controlled and accessed (versus centrally controlled and accessed) is not simply a technical detail under the domain of "user permissions." Decisions of these sorts can make an enormous difference in whether and how end users, like teachers, are able to see and assess student progress in digital education and review and use data generated by digital education platforms to better adapt instruction to students' needs.

This framework guided our analyses of specific cases of digital education, helping us hold in balance both the core of digital education (how it is experienced by students) and the larger questions of public/private or government/vendor influence in contracts for digital education. Much discussion of government contracts in public education focuses on issues of cost, service delivery, and other contract compliance issues. The framework introduced in figure I.1 is meant to supplement these compliance-oriented issues with more directed conversation around quality and access and how quality and access in digital education turn on vendors' decisions about instruction, curriculum, and data and assessment. The figure also highlights how these various elements interact with one another in the context of both the instructional setting and contracting process. The location of a particular vendor program model on the diagram is a function of where it sits on *all three axes* (curriculum, instruction, and data/assessment) in relationship to one another. For instance, the choice to not include a live instructor in a digital tutoring program may impact the ability to have locally controlled assessments.

We develop these ideas in the following chapters, including in chapter 6, where we show how practitioners and policy makers have leveraged these dynamics to begin a conversation about holding vendors more accountable for outcomes. While the *case*, or focus of our inquiry, is vendor influence in digital education, the challenges and strategies described are adaptable to other kinds of education contracting (e.g., charter schools, assessments) and public contracting outside of education.

These four central questions, as well as how they interact, also push us to seriously consider how the new products and services are serving low-income students. There is mixed evidence of students from low-income families being served well by digital education. This is not coincidental. Nor is it a sign that researchers aren't asking the right questions or aren't gathering the right data. It reflects instead the dangerous assumption that markets can solve social problems that governments cannot. The thinking is, "If only we just get out of the way and let competition and choice do its magic, the digital education market will work wonders for schools in low-income communities." We argue that this a dangerous assumption; the relationship between digital education and commercialism in schools is problematic and deserves careful scrutiny. Digital education pushes us deeper into the current that is breaking down the craft of teaching into ever smaller pieces—curriculum becomes a course for sale online or a video; teachers are part-time instructors/part-time data specialists; the grade book becomes the software the school leases from one vendor; and grades are online assessments leased from another vendor.

In order to get answers, we need to look upstream and downstream. In looking upstream we need to ask, *What purpose does education contracting serve in an era in which public schools have become more segregated spaces and the very idea of public schooling has come under increasing attack?* And in looking downstream we ask, *How are educators and local practitioners both responding to and altering the direction of these trends?* When we look upstream we see digital education growing through private-sector investment and government mandates, and we see online curriculum becoming a part of what is expected in schooling. We see technology being tied to ideals of standards-based reform, market-based reform, and personalized learning. When we look downstream, we see minimal data or evidence of effectiveness, lots of money being spent, and a deluge of gadgets pouring into schools with little emphasis on the capacity for teachers to use them or integrate them into the curriculum. And we see that these problems are as great, if not greater, in schools and programs that primarily serve low-income students.

So here we are again with a story that has played out repeatedly in education reform over the last century: the disconnect between the upstream policy makers' and CEOs' vision (technology can save our schools) and that of the downstream street-level practitioners (technology should be used only when it improves the quality of teaching and learning). What are we going to do? We can put our hands up and say, "Here we go again! What a mess!" and ask teachers to yet again take on these tensions and challenges as best they can. We can go with the tide pushing us toward contracting digital education without resisting and, yet again, leave schools serving low-income students with inadequate opportunities to learn in truly transformative instructional settings. We can swing in the other direction and adopt a singular view, rejecting digital education contracts as simply another attempt by corporations to take over public education.

Or we can engage in a critical, structured, and research-based dialogue about all of these ideas. Our vision behind this book is to say that there are places where we can stem the tide of fragmented, rushed, top-down approaches to digital education and capitalize on the strengths of the technology, people, and policies to think more deeply about how the digital era is changing the worlds of teaching and public policy.

We base our discussion of both the potential benefits and risks in contracting for digital education on the following interconnected points:

- *Digital education can be an asset for public schools and a critical part of addressing educational disparities for disadvantaged communities.* The potential lies in the use of technology for building higher-order thinking skills, increased access to data, and the construction of curriculum by teachers. This is, in principle, very good news for public schools. Not an anti–digital education argument, this current of thought instead looks at ways in which the relationships among policy makers, vendors, districts, teachers, parents, and students can be structured to ensure access to quality instruction and data.

- *Yet, there is a lack of accountability.* External providers are treated as merely technicians in all of this, when really they are making very important design decisions that shape how and what students learn. However, they are not being held accountable in the same ways that public schools and districts are. In order to hold the market more accountable to outcomes like greater equity and more equal distribution of digital education resources, we need transparency.

- *Digital education lacks transparency.* It is very difficult for the common citizen or teacher to see what is going on with the systems they are expected to use—who is being served, how much it is costing their school, what are add-on costs, and hidden commercialization (e.g., advertisements), not to mention what instruction actually looks like.

Combined, these currents contribute to a dynamic whereby the commercial and even policy imperatives for digital education may corrupt the theoretical potential of the technology as a transformative tool for teaching and learning, particularly in low-income settings.

* * *

In chapters 1 and 2 we frame the potential and problems of digital education—the increase in investor and policy activity and the potential to transform teaching, as well as the worrisome issues accompanying these trends, including the lack of a sound evidence base, the dominance of commercial imperatives, and evidence of a new digital gap still linked to economic disparities. In chapters 3–5 we follow these trends into schools, homes, and community settings where digital education occurs. First we examine a case of contracting for digital courses, describing contracting with districts for digital courses from the perspective of the vendor. Next we look at the first year of a public charter school contracting with a large digital curriculum vendor. And in the third case we examine contracting for digital tutoring where districts must contract with vendors to comply with mandates of No Child Left Behind. Building on these case studies, in chapter 6 we describe the tools that students, parents, and teachers (in partnership with districts) are using to make digital education more accountable to the people it is supposed to be serving in public schools. We close the book by circling back to the urgency of the issue and what is at stake, offering ways in which both upstream and downstream stakeholders can engage in structured dialogue around opportunities for quality digital education for low-income students.

PART ONE

Looking Upstream

CHAPTER 1

The Storm Surge in Digital Education and Privatization

IT IS 7:15 P.M. and a fifth grade student, Lynette, sits in the middle of the living room with her father. They have just finished turning this room of their modest one-bedroom apartment into a learning center for a scheduled online mathematics lesson starting at 7:30. Her father, a Zapotec man from the southern state of Oaxaca, Mexico, has ensured that the Internet connection is working properly, has set up a foldable table with enough scratch paper for his daughter to work with, and has opened the laptop (provided by a private vendor in order to complete the tutoring services) to the proper programs that the student will work on. This is their third session, and both are eagerly waiting for the instructor to log on from his or her remote location and begin the hour-long session.

The session runs into technical difficulties from the instructor's end and begins ten minutes late. The instructor begins by assigning the student twenty minutes of independent test-prep work. The program, however, runs into more technical difficulties and takes seven minutes to load. The student then answers multiple choice questions that are unaligned to both her current school work and grade level. Although her father's English proficiency is limited, he sits alongside her throughout the lesson and is showing some signs of unrest.

After the test-prep work, the one-to-one instruction begins. The instructor is either a voice or a presence acknowledged by instant messages displayed in the laptop. The instructor assigns Lynette a problem, but she mentions that she has already completed that specific problem. After three more attempts, the student begins to work on a word problem, which she answers in less than a minute. Her father helps. They both wait for the instructor to check the work and assign a new problem. The father is growing more concerned and visibly anxious. His daughter still has homework to finish. After nine minutes, the instructor texts the student, "Good job man!" He or she doesn't realize the student is a girl and hasn't asked. For the remaining twenty minutes, the student answers three questions. Most of the time is spent waiting. At 8:30 p.m., the instructor signs off.

This home digital instruction—engineered by a Silicon Valley start-up providing tutoring to Lynette and more than seven thousand low-income students in one of the largest urban school districts in the country—is precisely the sort of platform that policy makers and investors have identified as key to the future of public education. The challenges that Lynette faces are substantive and often typical for students and schools expected to use digital education to teach or learn. Policy makers at the federal, state, and local levels push to make online services and products the medium for everyday instruction, curriculum, and assessment. This policy push has been accompanied by an increase in public contracting for education services, as well as large corporate and philanthropic investments in new kinds of learning technologies. This technology may hold promise for improving quality and access in public education. However, the strong current of privatization has increasing influence on the direction of digital education. What gets taught via digital education, how it is taught, and how it is assessed often reflect the financial priorities of vendors (many of which are transnational companies) rather than the public interest in better access to high-quality schooling.

In the wake of No Child Left Behind (NCLB), policy makers increasingly have turned to digital education as a means to "fix schools." Digital education includes the use of technology in K–12 assessments and for the design and delivery of curriculum (such as e-textbooks) as well as the use of new hardware and software (e.g., tablets and digital education games) to instruct in classrooms. Digital education has surged upward on the national policy agenda in tandem with efforts such as the widespread adoption of the Common Core State Standards and the Race to the Top (RTT) initiative passed as part of American Recovery and Reinvestment Act (ARRA) of 2009. For instance, Digital Promise, a not-for-profit organization authorized into law through the Higher Education Act of 2007 and launched in 2011, recommends policies to increase the digital presence in schools and advocates for and encourages private and public investment and the use of digital innovations in public schools. It receives financial support from both public and private funders, including the U.S. Department of Education, the Carnegie Foundation of New York, and the Hewlett and Gates foundations, as well as various corporate partners such as Apple, Cisco Systems, and Pearson. The governing board is appointed by Secretary of Education Arne Duncan. In 2013, Digital Promise partnered with the Education Industry Association, the primary lobbying group for the education companies, to help streamline the district procurement process for purchasing educational technology and digital instruction for the public sector.

In another example, RTT authorized $350 million in government contracts for computerized assessments from two consortia, the Smarter Balanced Assessment System and the Partnership for Assessing Readiness for College and Careers (PARCC), specifically designed to develop computer-based products and services that would help states develop the interim and summative assessments required as part of RTT and the Common Core State Standards. In 2013, at the annual meeting of the American Education Researchers Association (AERA), Secretary Duncan described these two consortia as cornerstones of the Obama administration's education reform agenda:

> The new assessments from the consortia will be a vast improvement on assessment as it is done today. The PARCC consortium, for example, will evaluate students' ability to read complex texts, complete research projects, excel at classroom speaking and listening

assignments, and work with digital media. The Smarter Balanced Consortium will assess students using computer adaptive technology that will ask students questions pitched to their skill level, based on their previous answers . . . The use of smarter technology in assessments will also change instruction in ways that teachers welcome. Technology makes it possible to assess students by asking them to design products and experiments, to manipulate parameters, run tests and record data.

Duncan described digital education as an absolute "game changer for American education" and heralded the ability of Assessment 2.0, the post-NCLB digital-driven federal reform agenda, to transform instruction, curriculum, and assessment at every level of schooling: "I have no doubt that Assessment 2.0 will help educators drive the development of a richer curriculum and the state, district, and local level, differentiated instruction tailored to student needs, and multiple opportunities during the school year to assess learning."[1] The press on districts and states to buy or lease technology services and products is further reflected in President Obama's 2014 proposed education budget, which includes $65 million to create an Advanced Research Projects Agency (ARPA), "whose purpose is to invest in breakthrough research on STEM teaching and learning, with approximately $65 million for the Advanced Research Projects Agency for Education (ARPA-ED), which would allow the Department of Education to support high-risk, high-return research on next-generation learning technologies, including for STEM education."[2]

The federal government's public support of digital media comes alongside a long move toward digital education by investors and groups calling for a new generation of digital education media in schools.[3] For example, in 2011, under the direction of the Council of Chief State School Officers (CCSSO) and with funding from the Bill & Melinda Gates Foundation, the Shared Learning Collaborative (SLC) was formed, identified by its founders as "an alliance of states, districts, educators, foundations, and content and tool providers passionate about using technology to improve education."[4] The initial board of directors included Cheryl Vedoe, president and CEO of Apex Learning, one of the largest for-profit online content providers to public schools, and Randi Weingarten, president of the American Federation of Teachers.

Districts are feeling the pressure. They see reform initiatives, such as the implementation of the Common Core, as necessitating more outsourcing of instructional resources. For example, according to a survey by MDR, a provider of marketing information for education, as of 2013, 68 percent of districts plan to purchase new instructional materials as part of aligning to the Common Core, and the potential market for Common Core–related materials is 7,600 district buyers. Replacing textbooks with online resources was listed as a high to medium priority by 78 percent of curriculum directors, while procuring apps was a high to medium priority for 77 percent.[5]

These examples illustrate how public policy and corporate money intermingle to create conditions for increased procurement by districts and states of education services and products. The contracts are generating new sources of funds for vendors but also new kinds of organizations that are part public, part for-profit, and part philanthropic, such as Digital Promise. In these and other ways, contracting for digital education is moved downstream by broader changes in the very nature of public governance. In the United States, outsourcing of digital education is written into policy and reinforced in executive decisions. The organizations established to oversee contracts include representatives from both the technology industry and the public sector. With the establishment of these organizations, it is becoming less clear where the authorities of government and the education industry begin and end.

This rising tide of contracting for digital education comes as policy makers' conceptualizations and descriptions of digital education are increasingly conflated with the language and conceptions of the market. City and state officials across the nation describe their push toward technology in typical market-based terms, as investments that will pay off, reduce costs, and encourage innovation through competition. As in the case of NCLB, these ideas are paired with reference to current and long-standing public policy objectives, such as inclusive schooling for all students with learning disabilities or getting resources to all schools in ways that help "level in the playing field." For example, the idea of bringing virtual teachers into low-income settings translates into increasing the supply of highly qualified teachers in "hard-to-staff" schools. As the digital education market uses the language of public policy to sell products and services, government uses the language of the marketplace to sell the idea that digital education is a necessary component of implementing a national education agenda toward common and national standards and assessments.

Reinforcing this pressure from the federal level, some states and districts require that public schools use digital education, while others offer incentives (public funding) to get companies to sell public schools digital education. Indeed, state and federal governments and private schools were some of the first "investors" in opening online schools. However, for-profit entities have become primary drivers and financial beneficiaries of the venture, seeing the potential for enormous revenues. For example, Ohio's first online school, eCOT, is a statewide charter school operated by a for-profit company, and, as of 2013, it is the biggest online school in the state, with more than ten thousand students.

Districts such as New York City contract with for-profit companies to generate minute-by-minute data on student progress that is fed into company-designed algorithms and used to match teachers with students and students with lessons. Through supplemental educational services (SES) that fund the tutoring described in the vignette, districts across the nation contract with digital vendors of afterschool tutoring using federal funds.

The use of digital technologies enables the private sector to get inside public education in new ways. For example, as a function of SES contracts, digital tutoring vendors may inadvertently get access to students' individualized education plans, zip codes, and phone numbers. Districts contract with search engine companies to archive and manage access to thousands of lessons that teachers use to supplement textbook curriculum. As a function of these contracts, companies can gain access to students' consumer preferences, since the more the student uses a game portal, the more the company finds out about the student. Schools contract with vendors of online curriculum to meet state mandates requiring that students take an online course before they graduate. These companies leasing curricula to cyber schools then lobby state legislatures to expand online requirements and use projections of expanding enrollment in order to spur investor interest. As a function of these contracts, more students attend schools online, which may potentially lead to fewer students attending schools in public physical settings. These contracts draw on public funds used to support programs (focusing on class size reduction or early childhood education, for example) demonstrated by research to reduce the achievement gap.[6] This is particularly the case as public funds for special education technology programs have been cut due to state budget shortfalls.[7] As noted by Kevin Carey, the premise that there have been large increases in school funding over the past decade is overstated; the increases are largely explained by spending in special education.[8]

THE POTENTIAL OF DIGITAL EDUCATION

Digital education is a term we use to refer to the use of digital media explicitly for instructional purposes. This term encompasses a wide range of media, from digital games, to software used for formative and summative assessment for instructional purposes, to online short videos that teach math concepts. We organize our discussion around three types, or settings, of digital education in K–12 public education: (1) digital courses (both synchronous and asynchronous, which can be unit-specific or part of a fuller program) aimed at supporting students' regular school-day curriculum; (2) digital schools (blended learning schools and virtual schools) in which at least half of learning occurs online and supplants students' regular school-day curriculum; and (3) digital tutoring (online tutoring, credit recovery programs, and test preparation programs) aimed at supplementing or remediating students' regular school day curriculum. These categories are not intended to be exclusive; some forms of digital media (e.g., educational games) are used across settings.

This book is not a case *against* digital education. As this book goes to press, there is a strong set of arguments emerging around the potential of digital education to move us closer to pedagogical approaches that are antithetical to the drill-and-kill approach that descended rapidly with the standardized test emphasis of No Child Left Behind. The Common Core specifically references the use of digital education in support of higher-order thinking skills, a vision of learning that elevates the idea of strategic integration of technology in the classroom in order to help students use technology to produce, peer review, and publish their own writing, for example. A number of scholars have focused on the potential of digital education, such as digital games, to move us to a higher, exciting, new space for learning in public education.[9] In this space, powerful forms of learning built on principles of collaboration, discovery, and problem solving are made accessible to more students via technology. Think, for example, about a mathematics curriculum where students living in different corners of Los Angeles share data to weigh the risks and benefits of a company's attempts to install cell phone towers in their respective communities—using math while building argumentation skills. We are at a moment where we can think in much more concrete ways about how to integrate assessment into learning, into lessons, through software that lets students see their own progress and that rewards risk taking, and through games that teach us as we make mistakes. And there is a push in the Common Core to make skillful integration of technology in classroom instruction a criterion of quality instruction across all schools. For example, in the reading standards, students are expected to evaluate the advantages and disadvantages of using different media to present an idea.

We know that the potential is enormous. However, we think it is critical that at this moment we also examine how digital education may be changing public education in ways we don't always see. Digital education carries enormous risks for the kinds of schooling outcomes we care about, namely a democratic voice and more equitable distribution of resources. The risks are directly linked to the fact that while the digital education tide is rising, another tide is rising that views accountability in market-based terms. If you have competition and choice, the theory goes, everything else (e.g., innovation, equity) largely takes care of itself. The risks of digital education are perhaps as big or bigger than what we saw with NCLB: the commodification of learning via sale of testing products. The reason for this is that digital education can segment public education in ways that promote more selling and more commodification. It pushes us further into this dangerous current where teaching and learning get fragmented like grains of sand. It is not a textbook that is being sold; it is an entire curriculum that can operate, in principle, without a teacher. It is not just software for analyzing test score data; it is a system through which the very role of the teacher is transformed. The teacher becomes a kind of data specialist for whom the daily challenge is managing and digesting volumes of data that can make other critical aspects of teaching (explanation, modeling, encouragement) less possible. This selling of teaching and curriculum was happening long before digital education started to surge; the textbook industry was built around the principle that companies could make money off of curriculum. However, digital education splits the atom even further, splintering the very idea of public education into a wash of specialized functions, such as data mining, curriculum web crawling, and classrooms that are "live" for ten minutes.

The relationship between digital education and the narrative that education desperately needs to operate more like a market is significant and is frequently overlooked. It is a relationship that is hardening through a variety of factors, including laws that press schools to measure outcomes narrowly in terms of test scores and to do more with these outcomes on a shorter timeline. It also is conditioned by the fact that as the education marketplace evolves—with new things to sell to schools in new ways—so, too, do the organizations with enormous financial stakes in the digital services and products being sold.

Much of what is being placed on the market is exciting from an educator's point of view. The potential of digital education is enormous. Realizing this potential begins with acknowledging what we already know are critical learning conditions for low-income youth.[10] Research points to the following characteristics of high-performing schools serving low-income students:

- Certified and experienced teachers and principals
- High expectations for student achievement
- Coherent, standards-based curriculum and instruction
- Multiple forms of assessment data for the purpose of improving student achievement
- Up-to-date and supplementary instructional resources.[11]

Digital education can be transformative with regard to instruction. It can help support effective teaching practices, including recognizing and fostering existing student experiences and skills, building a curriculum that is relevant and responsive to students' lives, providing opportunities for students to apply their knowledge and skills to real-life situations, supporting the development of students' non-academic needs, facilitating active critical thinking and application over passive rote memorization, and tapping into student interests and intrinsic motivators.[12]

Research on how digital education can support these transformative goals through curriculum has found that it can create connected learning environments in which students become producers rather than consumers of media, connect with a broader group of people not bound by geography who share common purposes, and network diverse learning resources.[13] Digital education can create the space where new types of content can become a central part of the curriculum, such as video gaming and digital citizenship.[14] It has the potential to be highly structured and sequenced, particularly in the case of mathematics and science and, to some extent, language arts. It can give students in geographically isolated or low-income areas access to wider course offerings that might otherwise not be available, such as Advanced Placement and art classes.

Digital education also has the potential to be transformative in terms of building new and powerful assessment strategies. Through new technologies, the assessment feedback loop can be faster. A student completes an assignment and the results are sent to the teacher to help her better discern where the student needs help. Digital education and its technologies also create the opportunity for assessment data to be archived in a more structured way; there is a backup and structured record of student progress to which the teachers, parents, and students potentially have access.

While these possibilities in digital education have been widely discussed and publicized, they are not always happening in practice. Those examples of practitioners engaging in these potentially transformative practices are occurring in isolation rather than as a systemic feature of digital education.[15] According to leading educators working in the space, there is a lot of exciting innovation under way involving for-profits and not-for-profits, particularly in the digital gaming world.[16] However, particularly in the case of digital schools and curriculum, large-scale implementation of digital education is being directed by just a handful of national vendors that do not necessarily have a primary vested interest in developing transformative instruction. Sustained, systemic, transformative instruction involves investment in professional development; the content is more complex, and it demands an understanding of the research base supporting transformative practices.[17] In addition to commercial interests, much of digital education is being driven (consciously or not) by long-standing assumptions about what low-income children need, namely basic skill building over engaging and transformative instruction.[18] Digital education programs targeting low-income students thus do not generally come with built-in opportunities for transformative learning. In the words of one educator and former administrator of a digital school, the companies "simply don't get it."

We know that living in poverty is negatively associated with a child's prospects for school success. Living in poverty in early childhood contributes to lower rates of school completion.[19] We know that poverty rates for children are rising and that the percentage of children living in poverty is much higher for blacks (34 percent) and Hispanics (27 percent) than for Asians (11 percent) and whites (10 percent).[20] These real and persistent challenges to high-quality public schooling for students from low-income settings need to be front and center in public policy discussions about digital education. Certainly there are policy makers and practitioners who are doing this, who are trying to understand the potential and impact of digital education specifically for children living in poverty through its use by teachers in schools with high poverty rates. But much of the public discussion about digital education still is framed in terms of how remarkable the technology is and how it can be a "game changer," in the words of Arne Duncan, for students attending public schools. In reference to the realities of poverty and college-going rates (only 9 percent of low-income children are expected to get degrees), David Berliner argues that progressives rarely directly face the mythic qualities of the American Dream.[21] Inside of much education policy, argues Berliner, hide deep-rooted assumptions that individuals living in poverty should overcome the handicaps created by poverty. The assumption that low-income students can be educated into successful lives, absent larger social changes, doesn't become more plausible just because the reform has a new look (i.e., new technology or digital formats). Digital education may be seen as a cheaper and more efficient way to invest in educational programming in the context of shrinking budgets, but as many administrators will attest, truly transformative instruction is not cheap. In the absence of thoughtful oversight, digital education can have significant costs (time, missed opportunities) for those least able to afford them: teachers, students, and parents. Who isn't seeing or paying attention to this reality?

LOOKING UPSTREAM

In looking at the commercial and policy drivers behind the rise of digital education, we use *upstream* and *downstream* to frame our understanding of the fast currents of digital education and their effects on public schools. We still believe that what happens in schools, as well as classrooms and community centers, is critically important to whether and how well public schools serve historically disadvantaged students. Policies come alive through actions at the street level. Although downstream is where students and others make contact and engage with policy, the decisions made upstream still matter. Over the past several decades, leagues of researchers have tried to better understand how the culture of policy and schooling institutions shape educational practice. However, there hasn't been as much attention paid to how the work done upstream in the privatization of schools and the rise of education contracting makes its way downstream.[22]

The promise of digital education is heard everywhere. It is becoming part of the stream of expected practice in higher education, early childhood education, and schooling for students whose circumstances prevent them from attending regular public schools, such as homeless children, migrant children, youths in juvenile delinquent centers, children of military families, or youths who have dropped out of school. As activity around digital education increases, industry is becoming more organized to capture revenue from governmental purchase of digital education products and services.

In 2013 we attended the annual conference of the software industry association, held in the conference facilities of a hotel appropriately called The Palace in Silicon Valley, north of Los Angeles. The conference theme was Education Technology. It drew more than four thousand industry participants doing business in this area and was sponsored by some of the giants in the industry, companies such as Pearson, McGraw Hill, and other platinum sponsors. The price tag for the conference was high: $2,500.

We attended a session call Ed Tech 101 that was targeted for software start-ups looking to do business in the education space. It included companies such as ParentSquare, which was honored with the association's coveted Codie Award. This new company is building a business out of networking parents in the same classroom and creating pages that parents can control to keep track of their child's school progress. ParentSquare doesn't have paying customers, the twenty-something CEO reported to the session participants, but, in order to survive, it will need to start charging fees to parent users. The introduction of the fee signals the competitive pressures on education tech start-ups. It is the kind of fee that will likely be prohibitive for poor and working-class students, for whom home Internet access can be a luxury.

Industry representatives, such as the Education Industry Association (EIA), are working hard to increase their access to public funds, as reflected in an initiative launched in 2012 by EIA called Private Ventures for the Public Good:

EIA and the Education Foundation Initiative are carrying out a long-term comprehensive advocacy, research, professional development and communications campaign that aims to create a fairer and more open market in which the private sector may compete on equal footing with public school districts and non-profit organizations to provide solutions to teaching and learning in PreK–12 education. If the campaign is successful, no longer will the "for-profit" moniker routinely precede descriptions of education companies, and consumers of publicly funded education will have real options in selecting from among diverse providers of high-quality services and products.[23]

EIA created a not-for-profit, 501(c)(3), the Education Industry Foundation (EIF), to "support the role of private enterprise in PreK–12 education," including raising unrestricted funds and providing research support for the Private Ventures for the Public Good campaign.[24] While this information campaign launched by EIA references the public good, its mission is primarily commercial. EIA and the efforts of EIF represent some of the biggest private providers of digital education, including Pearson, which dominates the digital education market both in the United States and internationally.

A Global Market

For companies such as Pearson, digital education is a global market. In places like India and Brazil, with their emerging economies, "edupreneurs" such as Samudra Sen of LearningMate are doing billions of dollars of education technology business across forty countries and are now looking to enter the U.S. market. At the same time, many large U.S. companies are reaping returns on investments in education technology. In India, unlike the United States, there are laws against running education-based companies on a for-profit basis. However, in India spending on education (by parents) is second only to spending on food; for example, in government-funded schools tablets are distributed (for a purported price tag of $15) to students with curricula loaded onto to it. Transnational companies also are selling technology products and services to teachers from one end of the globe to another. Companies such as Zondle, based in New Zealand, have built a paying customer base in software that lets teachers create their own content and play their own games. Zondle executives track demand for their product in part through the user statistics, which, according to one report, moved from 1.5 million to 6.5 million users over the course of six months, with most of the upsurge happening in the U.S. market.

Political changes in other countries have pushed demand for contracting up to the national level. Political elites in Australia have used economic crises to press for a major review of school funding. A new national curriculum to be phased in over the course of nine years is expected to be the catalyst for the emergence of a digital education marketplace in Australia. The curriculum will be delivered entirely online, stimulating an expanding federal role in investment in technology devices and infrastructure. This new curriculum will increase dollars paid to education technology businesses and investors mostly outside of Australia, particularly U.S. companies.

Investor Activity in the United States

Corporate activity in education in emerging world markets is shaping political arrangements and spheres of support for education technology in the United States. The influence of philanthropies such as the Gates Foundation and the flow of money from investors funding digital education products and services are increasing, even as schools themselves face hard times financially. Investor activity is an important indicator and facilitator of the expansion of online learning. In an interview with *Education Week* in February 2012, Adam Newman, a founding partner of Education Growth Advisors, remarked, "I have not seen this level of investor interest in the K–12 business in the last decade by any stretch of the imagination. What you have right now in K–12 education is an ecosystem of really dynamic entrepreneurs and emergent companies and a very diverse set of organizations that have become interested in the education space."[25]

Over the past decade, education investors' investments in education technology in the United States were estimated at $146 million in 2002; by 2011 this number had nearly tripled, reaching $429 million.[26] Most of the money in sales and acquisitions in K–12 education from 2000 to 2011 was in the education technology sector. In recent years this sector accounted for more than half of the transactions related to K–12 education. Some transactions from 2011 show the scale of this business: Pearson purchased SchoolNet for $230 million, and K12 Inc. purchased Kaplan Virtual Education, which runs virtual education programs for public and private schools in nine states, for $13 million.[27] Blackboard Inc., which specializes in online learning management platforms, was purchased by the Providence Equity Group in 2011 for $1.64 billion. In 2012, Apple partnered with the three largest textbook publishers—Pearson, McGraw-Hill, and Houghton Mifflin—to offer e-textbooks exclusive to the iPad.[28]

As further indication of K–12 technology's popularity as a business endeavor, investors in the Chicago and New York City school districts are vying to be the epicenter of the K–12 education industry. In a blog posted on November 26, 2012, Tom Vander Ark, a partner in Learn Capital, one of the major investors in education technology, argued that "New York City Schools have been the most innovative in the country, NYC is home to most education industry leaders and the second most prolific tech start-up and Edtech hot spot on the planet." His blog lists some of the most notable education start-ups in New York City, including Socratic Labs, Late Nite Labs, Chalkable, Knowledge Delivery Systems, Unbound Concepts, and Learn Bob.[29]

In response to Vander Ark's posting, Christopher Nyren, whose professional profile includes strategizing for the Apollo Group, the largest for-profit education company in the world, responded on November 29, 2012, "In fact, New York can only rank as high as the third most prolific EdTech hotspot on the planet," arguing that, "for over a generation now, Chicago has served as the epicenter of for-profit technology-enabled education, entrepreneurship, and investment." He identifies Chicago as the birthplace of online learning and notes that two Chicago-based ed tech companies, Embanet Compass and Delta, were recently sold for five times what they posted in revenue.[30]

These comments, and the competitive environment that prompted them, reflect the increasing cachet of digital education among technology investors. Investors are pouring money into start-ups that can capitalize on growing enrollments in online learning. Particularly popular are companies that will be able to contract with school districts or states around the software required to run and operate online and blended learning courses and schools. For example, in 2009 First Mark Capital invested $20 million in Knewton, a start-up launched in 2008 that specializes in platforms that link technology to formative and summative data, which, in principle, allow students and teachers to get real-time data on test score performance. Students complete a test and immediately get data on the percentage of answers correct, all without the teacher. Teachers can compare student performance on test items as students are taking the test and generate reports for daily planning purposes. Similarly, in 2011, Union Square Ventures invested $2.5 million in CodeAcademy, which specializes in online courses in computer programming, where students earn badges and, eventually, course credits for learning computer programming. In 2012, Expansion Venture Capital spent $1.3 million to kick-start Chalkable, a company that collects curriculum, assessment, and instruction content and curates it on a web-based platform.

From a business standpoint, it makes sense to invest in companies that can eventually sell to districts. According to the Center for Education Statistics, K–12 education spending rose from $524 billion to $544 billion in 2011–2012.[31] It is projected that by 2015 $21 billion will be spent on technology, up from the $16 billion spent on technology in 2010. In 2013, 89 percent of districts reported that they spent the same or more than the previous year on technology, and 87 percent reported that they spent the same or more on curriculum, including educational software. As of 2011, 63 percent of districts with enrollments larger than 10,000 students contracted with an outside organization to provide online courses.[32]

Increased Technology in Public Schools

As investors put more money into education companies and as education companies put new digital education services and products on the market, public schools consume more technology. Since 1994, the National Center on Education Statistics (NCES) has surveyed representative samples of approximately 1,000 public schools on whether they have Internet access and, since 1996, on the types of Internet connections they use. In 2000, NCES reported that the percentage of public schools connected to the Internet had increased from 35 percent in 1994 to 95 percent in 1999.[33] The percent of instructional rooms with Internet access in public schools also increased during the same time period from 3 percent to 63 percent. From 1998 to 1999, the ratio of students to computer dropped slightly from twelve to nine students per computer.

In 2010, NCES published the findings from its annual survey of public schools to track access to information technology in schools and classrooms.[34] It found that 97 percent of teachers had one or more computers in the classroom every day, while 54 percent could bring computers into the classroom. Internet access was available for 93 percent of the computers located in the classroom every day and for 96 percent of the computers that could be brought into the classroom. The ratio of students to computers in the classroom continued to drop to approximately five students to every one computer. Teachers also reported that they or their students used computers in the classroom during instructional time often (40 percent) or sometimes (29 percent). Teachers stated that they or their students used computers in other locations in the school during instructional time often (29 percent) or sometimes (43 percent). These findings are buttressed by a recent report from the 2013 Pew Internet and American Life Project which found that 92 percent of the 2,462 (mostly public school) teachers surveyed said that the Internet has had a "major impact" on their ability to access content materials and other resources for teaching.[35] The teachers also reported that the Internet has had a "major impact" on their interactions with parents (67 percent) and students (57 percent).

An important test of expansion in digital education is the rate of attendance in full-time online schools. In 2001, one estimate placed the number of secondary students taking one or more distance education courses at 40,000–50,000 students.[36] Just ten years later, 6 million students were taking at least one online course.[37] The Evergreen Institute estimated a 16 percent increase in enrollment in virtual classes at the K–12 level between the 2010–2011 and 2011–2012 school years.[38] Virtual school providers also increased enrollment. The leading U.S. provider of online schooling, K12 Inc., increased its enrollment from 2009 to 2010 by 22 percent.[39]

The number of states requiring some form of online education is also growing. As of 2011, 40 states had some kind of statewide K–12 online learning option, up from 30 states in 2007; and 31 states and the District of Columbia had statewide full-time online schools, up from 18 states in 2007. There are also a few school districts now using online education as a condition of graduation. In 2012, Idaho and Virginia passed legislation that required students to take an online course in order to graduate, and Minnesota passed a law that strongly encourages, not requires, students to take an online course. Alabama, Florida, and Michigan have required an online course for graduation since 2010, with Michigan's law requiring that students finish twenty hours of online learning in order to graduate, accruing hours as early as sixth grade.[40]

School districts in general similarly enrolled large numbers of students in online courses. Of the approximately 1,816,400 enrollments in online learning courses (not including full-time online schools) in 2009–2010, 74 percent were high school students. This represents a tremendous expansion in online enrollments in 2000, when it was estimated that 40,000–50,000 students were enrolled in K–12 online courses. According to one estimate, the primary reason school districts are offering online learning opportunities is to provide courses not otherwise available at their schools and for credit recovery (for classes missed or failed). Some districts have created special shadow districts for online education, such as the Innovation Zone, or Izone, in New York City, which offers credit recovery and Advanced Placement courses as well as online afterschool tutoring test preparation in English and mathematics at the elementary school level.[41]

New Commercial Spaces in Schools

The World Wide Web, GoogleBrain, and Apple have contributed to the rising tide of education technology in schools. The changes began in the 1980s when Apple made a computer that cost less than $2,000. According to an industry insider, Apple opened the door for digital education through a marketing strategy that made it easier for schools to see how and why their work would be made easier through computers. Vendors approached the secretary rather than the principal and established a price point that wouldn't require approval from higher-ups. Soon Apple was one of the biggest sellers to schools and had started Apple School and a web page for educators.

When the world moved online in the late 1990s, entirely new markets opened up with the demand for online services and products that could help schools signal compliance with NCLB and avoid sanctions. As the technology evolved, so did the products and services. Computer-based testing gave way to full-service learning management systems that allowed different kinds of users (administrators, teachers, students, and parents) to log into a common system and access a range of updated content. About the same time, some of the bigger industry players (e.g., K12 Inc. and Pearson) began acquiring technology companies inside and outside the private sector and creating markets for "new kinds of schools," first termed "digital schools" and "cyber schools." By 2013 Pearson was selling more than 140,000 different instructional products and services, with a majority of them accessed online, and K12 Inc. was running virtual schools that used a common platform and were operated worldwide. As of 2013, medium to large districts that might once have only purchased the computer were now paying six figures for annual subscriptions to online lesson planners. Companies selling these kinds of products, such as Big Universe Learning, were posting over $8 million in revenues.

As competition in the market intensified, companies pushed digital education into new spaces. What was once organized and delivered in person, typically by government employees, could now be bought online and delivered to teachers and students directly through the web. For instance, there is a growing market for online professional development that replaces the tradition of professional development days or late summer orientation. Also, districts pay headhunters to recruit, vet, and relocate teachers, all online. Some districts are even purchasing third-party applications to track Internet use among students and teachers, which allow districts to cut off network access in schools and thereby maintain students' focus during periods of standardized testing. And companies such as BrainPop and Khan Academy are developing and archiving lesson content online and selling it to districts experimenting with flipped classrooms, where the student is expected to view the video lesson first and then go into class and discuss the content.

On the heels of new products and services have come new marketing strategies and new forms of organization linked to these strategies. A thirty-year veteran of the textbook industry who has worked for every major publisher told an audience of education start-up executives at the software industry's 2013 annual education technology conference that going to association meetings (the National Council of Teachers of Mathematics, the National School Boards Association, and others) was, in 2013, a waste of time and resources. The resources, he argued, were better spent on "developing a web presence" that administrators might stumble on or be directed to via Google or other search engines that compile information on users. For vendors interested in making the sale, the content of the website is supposedly as important as, if not more than, the design of the actual product. On their websites companies post testimonials, sample lesson plans, and links to other kinds of information that school staff might find useful. The websites are designed to provide the company with more leads and potential customers; whenever a teacher or administrator follows a link or downloads a paper, it provides the company with more information. The goal, as one education technology marketing consultant argued, is not necessarily to just get districts to buy your product but to get district administrators to see you as a source of information to which they will return again and again and possibly refer to others, whose peek at your website then provides even more information and possible entries into other markets.

The tools used in this marketing strategy, which some refer to as digital tagging systems, have helped create more products and services that technology companies can sell to schools and districts. In a reform climate with a laser focus on performance, administrators are starting to buy software that can help them gauge student and worker participation and productivity. These tools can monitor when and how frequently students and teachers access a program and at what times of the day. Virtual schools can identify which full-time teachers are not logging into the company's networks as much as they should. In these and other ways, the surge in digital education isn't just changing what schools do; it is changing how staff across schools and those who supervise them transmit data and information about schools and their employees, what these administrators can see and control and what they can't. These dynamics generate new policy issues around data privacy and access. For example, the Family Education Rights and Privacy Act (FERPA) prohibits the disclosure of students' protected information to a third party, such as vendors. However, under current FERPA regulations, there is much room for interpretation about whether students taking courses online are covered by FERPA, as they don't attend class in person.[42]

The rights of students and families, while protected by law, are complicated by power asymmetries as transnational media giants such as Google become more involved in the business of student information. There is now Google School, Google School Information System, and Google Apps for Education, which offers educators free access to a suite of services and products for collaborating through e-mail and the cloud. Students conduct group projects via these apps and teachers use them to instruct and respond to these and other assignments. Google also offers free instructional tools to educators, where it serves as a kind of accreditation agency. It offers online training programs that vet and certify teachers as "Google Teachers," who then become part of Google's free Certified Trainer Directory.[43]

In principle, all of this is happening to increase access and participation among high-poverty students. For example, we have the technology to monitor how teachers are using other technology. We also have the technology to identify when students, and which students, including those from high-poverty settings, use digital education—when they log in, how long they spend on a course, and what they are not getting. Curiously, however, the industry and policy makers have not yet leveraged technology in ways that help us better understand whether and how teachers and students access this data and use it toward more responsive instruction and alignment with state standards. In fact, the very industry which claims that its software will address the opportunity gap has on occasion identified low-income students as undeserving of technology. For example, the CEO of Udacity, a company specializing in online remedial math, explained low participation rates in the program as the students' problem rather than industry's problem, stating, "These were students from difficult neighborhoods, without good access to computers, and with all kinds of challenges in their lives . . . It's a group for which this medium (digital education) is not a good fit."[44]

Thus, from a vendor's perspective, the perceived value of digital education and digital tagging is first and foremost commercial. It comes from the first sale, the swipe of the credit card or the cutting of the check. It also comes from the information that the company gathers on educators as part of the sale and the information that they can track about the customer as he or she uses the product or service. This information can be used by customers (e.g., districts) to measure student or teacher performance, but it also can be used by businesspeople to sell more products and target new customers.

DIGITAL EDUCATION AS A FORM OF CONTRACTING

In looking upstream, the influence of larger political agendas behind the surge becomes evident. Education contracting has a long history in the United States. Before the 1990s, contracting for services in K–12 education focused primarily on textbooks or noninstructional services such as transportation and food services. However, with the new millennium, outside vendors—both for-profit and not-for-profit—have become designers, deliverers, and evaluators of the daily operation and provision of public education. This engagement is readily apparent in large urban school districts that are contracting with vendors for services such as school management for traditional and charter schools.[45]

Less evident is the sale of specialty educational products and services such as assessment services, professional development training, and afterschool tutoring.[46] In 2010, roughly $80 billion of the $750 billion state and federal dollars spent on public education (pre-K to higher education) went to outside organizations for products and services that both complement and supplement basic education services.[47] The involvement of outside organizations in providing services, in what is a public function of government and largely relying on public dollars, is a form of what some refer to as *privatization,* an umbrella term for "increased reliance on private actors and market forces to pursue social goals."[48]

Building on a prior conceptualization as described by Katrina Bulkley and Patricia Burch, we understand that the roles and relationships of government and vendors in education contracting vary along spectra.[49] Education contracting varies in terms of *what* is being contracted, from instructional to noninstructional services. It also varies in terms of the *role of the vendor,* from assistive with limited influence to highly controlling with heavy influence. The *role of government* in overseeing the contract also varies, from limited to heavy oversight.

Digital education as a case of government contracting doesn't fit neatly on a continuum. It is both the next chapter of education contracting and a critical moment in that steady stream of government outsourcing of public education. For example, digital education can include highly specialized services, such as contracts for math assessment software for special education students, and can also provide full-school management, as in the case of public online schools, where public schools contract with vendors for practically everything needed to run a school, from assessment software to online curriculum to tablets and computers on which instruction is delivered. As in the case of Pearson, a multinational media company, one vendor can be the go-to vendor for a district for all kinds of services, specialized and full management, instructional and noninstructional.

One vendor can hold a monopoly over school operations in an entire district, providing everything from computer-based assessments to management technology for tracking procurements and district costs. Although a district still has control over its operations—it develops the RFPs and pays the vendors—vendors have heavy influence on instructional policy through simultaneous contracts for assessments and full-school management. If what gets tested gets taught, then the vendor that has a monopoly in computer assessments will have the monopoly in instruction. The vendor controlling the assessment market also controls the school management market. The computer-based assessments help set the standard for what counts as school progress and improvement. Schools that do poorly on the assessment are targeted for closure, creating the space for new kinds of schools (e.g., online schools, blended learning schools) and, in turn, new sales for the vendor.

Education contracting also varies in terms of how involved the provider is in the work of school operations—or along the continuum of control as described by DiMartino, from vendors who play merely an assistive role to vendors who control most of school operations.[50] But in education contracting, as in other forms of contracting, a product or service can change hands frequently and involve many different layers. This is particularly likely in digital education, because technology segments instruction into smaller bits and pieces. There is no longer just the textbook. There is the virtual platform through which the curriculum is accessed, the online tutor who presents much of the content, and the digitized assessment system aimed at providing interim and summative feedback. Governments contract with vendors to run digital schools; some digital schools contract with content providers for their curriculum. Charter schools have their own contracts with digital course providers; the district or state contracts with a management organization to run online charter schools. Some digital education is meant to supplant regular school-day curriculum (in the case of virtual schools), while other varieties are designed to supplement it (as in the case of digital games or afterschool digital tutoring). The layers of activity can obscure a vendor's actual role and influence in a district. Even in settings where there isn't a monopoly, vendors are everywhere, moving into and out of different contracts within and across districts.

Education contracting also varies in terms of the extent to which the government agency (e.g., the school or district) manages the contract. In some cases, there may be little oversight and the vendor is left to do what it pleases. In other cases, there may be a lot of oversight, with the vendor having to demonstrate actively that it is making good on what it promised in the contract. Contracting for digital education also can make it difficult to see how much oversight is occurring. Take the case of digital afterschool tutoring that we explore further in chapter 5, where a district might contract with a digital vendor to provide afterschool tutoring online. The district is responsible for making sure that the vendor delivers what it describes in the contract. However, the district doesn't have access to the digital curriculum in the same way it does when it contracts for education services delivered in school settings. It has to get permission from the vendor to log in and see what the vendor is actually offering students and teachers.

Whose Interests Does Contracting Serve?

The passage of NCLB opened the floodgates to vendors interested in doing business with schools. In 2013 the future of NCLB was still being debated, but there were few signs of a slowdown in contracting for instructional services. The marketplace of accountability has stuck and helped strengthen interest groups devoted to the cause. Company executives appear to be very optimistic about the possibilities of a growing education market in the K–12 space. The political strategies of these organizations have matured as they knit goals of commercialism to accountability. The rise and adoption of Common Core State Standards has created new alliances and forms of organization. In May 2013, as states such as California hustled to roll out the Common Core, we received a letter from Steven Pines, the director of the Education Industry Association (EIA):

> I am pleased to let you know of a new EIA partnership with the American Association of School Administrators (AASA), which

represents over 13,000 school district superintendents. EIA will recommend high quality suppliers of school services and products, who are in good standing with EIA, for the AASA School Solutions Center the go-to resource used by district buyers when they seek vendors. This is the first-time the School Solutions Center will promote instructional services, ed-tech solutions and academic products. Accepted companies may promote this AASA connection to local district decision-makers and AASA will make door-opener introductions on your behalf. In addition, vendors receive booth space at the annual conference and are highlighted in AASA publications to their membership.

The major interest group representing education providers has a partnership with the major professional association representing school districts. The interest group works with policy makers to create commercial opportunities for education vendors inside of districts. The interest group identifies for the district which providers are "high quality," thus setting standards for the government for provider effectiveness. These kinds of alliances are part of the continued rise and legitimation of the outsourcing of education services and products. The contracting industry is becoming more closely wedded to public policy—in this instance, standards of quality and effectiveness.

The rise of education contracting comes at a time of political change, including mounting criticism of public agencies and calls for more accountability and transparency. These years in which digital education is surging, building in the wake of NCLB, represent a unique moment in public education, a time when calls for public accountability and, to some degree, corporate accountability, are on the rise. For instance, the 2012 campaign speeches of President Barack Obama and Senator Elizabeth Warren of Massachusetts called for greater transparency and accountability on the part of large corporations historically considered "too big to fail." In 2008 they had failed and, as the facts unfolded, failed as a choice and in ways that would boost executives' fortunes while leaving children and families across the country struggling with foreclosure, no or inadequate health care, and teacher shortages. But in 2013 there was still little bite to corporate accountability policy and oversight. Industry lobbying, huge campaign contributions, and the investment banking industry continued to dictate policy in Washington, and proposals for get-tough approaches to transparency in the corporate sector and banking reforms were sidelined by the president and Congress.[51]

Some would argue that corporations and contracts govern themselves. The assumption is that the competitive nature of the market will govern the actions of vendors; they will create the best product and the lowest price, because if they don't a competitor will get their bid. However, research on contracting tells a different story.[52] Across diverse services, from garbage collection to prison management, contracting seems to generate many more problems than it solves. The vendors aren't "governing" very well, and the services aren't improving. As Carolyn Heinrich concludes:

> Third party governance confronts its most onerous challenges in areas where service technologies are more complex and highly specialized (or asset specific) and thus measuring or monitoring performance in terms of both quality and efficiency are more difficult; there are too few suppliers (or providers) to assure a competitive market for services, government capacity for effectively managing relationships that are decentralized or devolved is limited and/or implementation is hampered by resource (time and funding) constraints and policy goals and directives are vague and not agreed on by all parties.[53]

Further, when governments decide to outsource functions otherwise performed in-house, vendors get more than money; they get more influence in public policy. The vendors get paid for doing something that public agency employees would otherwise do and then, either by law or de facto, tend to also get some control and authority over what people signing up for or requiring these services actually get. In government contracting, vendors can get more power and authority without having to be held accountable to the public or to the people supposed to benefit from government programs. In these and other ways, government contracts may not deliver, and there doesn't seem to be much movement inside or outside of education to push corporate accountability forward.

The assumption that markets' innovations will eventually reach low-income students and that they will benefit from them is unfounded. In fact, the reverse is true. Decades of research suggest that market-based reforms absent government oversight do not serve the interests of students in poverty. Without wise and active public governance, market-based reforms will *not* serve the interests of students who lack financial resources and will *not* serve the interests of students who require additional financial resources for transformative education.[54]

Make or Buy Digital Education?

Contracts for education follow these general trends in contracting. Although the equation might change in the future, for now government agencies are under increasing pressure to purchase digital education. The technologies are new and changing rapidly, and it is hard for public agencies to keep up. Whether to make or buy becomes a kind of forced choice. Put differently, while every public agency has a technology department, those offices don't specialize in *developing* technology, like software companies do, just as school districts don't usually publish textbooks. They contract for digital school services and products. And, as might be expected, as the number of these contracts grow, so do the power and influence of particular vendors.

Online vendors that serve thousands of students across large urban areas make decisions about services that reflect their interest in keeping their market share, particularly if they are for-profit vendors. They are in the business of selling software or hardware and yet are making important decisions that seem to take on roles previously assumed by governments. In the digital space, this means deciding which students have access to the software and hardware and which do not, what the purpose and role of the teacher is, what kind of training and support teachers deserve or need, how much time students get to spend on curriculum, and how students are assessed.

WHERE WE STAND NOW

Digital education is no longer a trickle in public schools. It is moving rapidly downstream at storm-level intensity. It is coming, say some vendors and policy makers, whether schools are ready or not. There is promise in digital education, but given some claims that digital education is a lifeline for public schools, the picture remains very muddy. These combined currents contribute to a dynamic whereby the commercial and even policy imperatives for digital education corrupt the theoretical potential of the technology as a transformative tool for teaching and learning. Believing in that potential makes sense. Buying it without evidence is something quite different.

CHAPTER 2

Faulty Assumptions

How Market Models of Accountability Undercut the Potential of Digital Education

DIGITAL EDUCATION HOLDS great promise for transforming teaching and learning. But as yet it is falling short of this promise, especially in schools with predominately low-income students, who still have unequal access to high-quality technology relative to their higher income peers.

Investor activity in digital education is high, with new digital services and products appearing daily. "There's an app for that" applies to education, too. For example, there is now an app that parents can use to check their children's grades, provided that their school has adequate bandwidth and that the parent owns a smart phone and has Internet access.

Without systematic attention to the issue of unequal resources, high-quality digital technology will be spread unevenly across communities, with economic privilege breeding technological privilege.[1] Part of the problem lies in a lack of accountability and transparency on the part of those providing digital education. And one of the main reasons we have this problem is that market models of accountability generally still assume that deregulation and unfettered markets will fix everything and, in this instance, bring more value to students than face-to-face schooling.

In this chapter we dig deeper into the problems of accountability and transparency in digital education. While there certainly is enormous potential for digital education to be an asset to public schools and teachers, to date there is very limited research that suggests that online courses alone add value or are a better alternative to face-to-face schooling. And there is growing evidence which suggests that there are economic disparities in access to innovations in digital education.

THE ROLE OF POLICY AND PROFIT IN PUSHING DIGITAL EDUCATION

Public policy is creating demand for digital education in a variety of ways. First, policy is working in the interest of the digital education market through mandates requiring that it be a part of the standard curriculum for particular students and/or for particular schools. Just as an increasing number of states require some form of online education, more and more school districts also are mandating online learning for particular groups of students. These courses sometimes supplement, but in other instances supplant (replace completely), students' regular curriculum. For example, in 2010, the Los Angeles Unified School District (LAUSD) required an online math curriculum for all ninth graders taking Algebra 1.[2] The district contracted with a third-party vendor, Quick and Associates, which has a subcontract with the curriculum developer, Assessment and Learning in Knowledge Spaces (ALEKS), to manage the program. Quick and Associates promised LAUSD "special pricing" as part of the deal, with ALEKS offering the district subscriptions at $28 per student per year. What the firm lost in revenue from the price cut, it made up five-fold in the number of subscriptions; as of 2013, there were approximately 66,000 ninth graders enrolled in LAUSD, 65 percent of whom were enrolled in Algebra 1. The contract is not publically available, but we can estimate that it is worth over a $1 million.

These state and local online course mandates are generating significant revenue for corporations and are also serving to alter the funding structure and redirect funding streams toward digital education. States and local school districts can pay for these contracts though tuition based on average district attendance (ADA). In some states, like California, there are restrictions on the use of these funds, such as a minimum amount of face-to-face instruction. However, in other states, such as Arizona, these restrictions have been eliminated, creating more political and commercial space for online companies to sell instruction online for the district at cost. For example, in 2011 Arizona lifted the caps on limits to the number of online charter schools that can provide statewide courses. By law, any school or district can set up online programs. After the policy change, the number of online schools approved by the state jumped from fourteen to sixty-six. Much of the revenue from the operation of these schools found its way to for-profits such as K12 Inc., which in 2011 earned $12.8 million profit from $522 million in revenue, 85 percent of which came from its online services.

Policy can also create demand for digital education through incentive programs. For example, in 2013 the Federal Communications Commission proposed an overhaul and expansion of its $2.3 billion program to provide schools with up-to-date telecommunications service and equipment. The proposal included measures that could help reduce the cost of contracting for digital education, such as the adoption of purchasing consortiums that would allow districts to pool funds to purchase the bandwidth required to effectively run many of the new digital education programs.[3]

And policy can create demand for digital education through competitive grants that make possible the purchase of assessment systems necessary for compliance with national reforms. For example, in 2010 the Department of Education awarded four-year grants, each over $170 million, to WestEd and Achieve to design and manage large-scale assessment systems linked to the Common Core State Standards.[4] The Partnership for Assessment of Readiness for College and Careers (PARCC, managed by Achieve Inc.) and the

Smarter Balanced Assessment Consortium (SBAC, managed by WestEd) were described in policy memos as voluntary membership organizations composed of states that have adopted the Common Core. The new assessment systems were based on requirements from the U.S. Department of Education that students take performance-based assessments for accountability, that the assessment system be computer based for the intended purposes of "more sophisticated design and quick reliable reporting," and that the systems follow requirements related to the kind and manner in which data is reported. Through the new assessment systems, states were expected to monitor whether students were on track with the standards. This data would then be used to pinpoint problem areas, such as schools or teachers requiring intervention. And in this era of accountability reforms, what is taught also gets tested, and the web (and those who make money from it) is now a primary means through which all student assessment flows. These kinds of policies push states and districts to invest and typically contract out for software and hardware. For example, both the PARCC and Smarter Balanced systems require online summative testing, with the PARCC system requiring summative testing at various points in the year and the Smarter Balanced system requiring summative assessments the last twelve weeks of the school year. PARCC's system requires 100 percent computer scoring for the summative assessment with a one-week turnaround time for results. Test scoring under the Smarter Balanced system combines human and computer scoring in the testing used for accountability. The computer elements of the system are directly linked to student, school district, and state-level accountability. The scores generated by computer-based assessments are used to determine students' scores on tests and proficiency rates. With the adoption of the Common Core by most states, the "old" assessments are becoming obsolete.

In principle, according to mainstream contracting theory, districts and states will buy rather than make when the "product" or "service" is new and in the development phase. Under these conditions, so goes the theory, governments will purchase rather than make because it is more cost-effective. Through the comprehensive assessment system, the federal government presents districts with a forced choice; they have little option but to join a voluntary organization managed (through a very large contract) by third-party vendors that then subcontract with software companies to design and manage the comprehensive assessment systems that perform all of the sophisticated computer-based assessment activities specified by federal law. In the case of mandates for online learning, policy assigns vendors a critical niche in the instructional space. In the case of Race to the Top and the Common Core, federal policy also gives outside vendors a critical role in designing and driving assessment. In both instances, public funds are being used to essentially create (e.g., PARCC and Smarter Balanced) new big vendors and organizations or to bankroll existing vendors (e.g., ALEKS) through large contracts.

Policy also works in the interest of digital education markets when policy leaders link digital education to broader common goals, such as closing the opportunity gap or cutting costs. In a State of the Union address in 2011, President Obama made the link between education, technology, and economic competitiveness: "We need to win the future by out-innovating, out-educating, and out-building our global competition." Obama administration appointees repeated and developed the specificity of this agenda. At a conference at Harvard University in March 2011, Deputy Secretary of Education Tony Miller stated, "Education reform and our global competitiveness depend on all of us embracing innovative ideas and technologies." In a talk at the South by Southwest Education Conference in Austin, Texas, Secretary Arne Duncan noted that "the future of education includes a laptop on every desk and universal Internet access in every home."[5] He pushed the product pitch further on the campaign trail in 2012: "I have been very public that we need to move from print to e-readers as fast as we can." He did it again more forcefully in his keynote speech at the annual meeting of education researchers in San Francisco in 2013, referring to the post-NCLB, next-generation federal policy agenda as Assessment 2.0, a term that explicitly links the Common Core State Standards to digital education.[6] At a briefing on the federal proposal to change the E-Rate system, President Obama established the goal of connecting 99 percent of school students to the Internet through high-speed broadband and high-speed wireless access in five years. Remarking at the briefing, he said that to meet this goal "we have to build connected classrooms that support modern teaching investments that we know our international competitors are already making."[7]

The idea that public education *needs* digital education is reinforced and promulgated through the messages of policy leaders who, in blogs, posts, white papers, essays, and articles, further the idea that the problem of schools is that they are organized, staffed, and resourced in all the wrong ways—and digital education can help change that. In other words, digital education is not just a means to improved instruction; it becomes a means to restructure schools in ways that more closely align them with corporate principles of accountability. Indeed, the Obama administration's assertion that digital education has a major role in improving our public school system has many influential supporters.

The far-reaching digital education movement includes alliances and groups that might otherwise disagree sharply on the purposes of education. Some of the most dominant voices in the discourse are from the tech industry, individuals like Michael Horn of the Innosight Institute and Tom Vander Ark of Learn Capital, who described digital education primarily in terms of the ebbs and surge of the market and equated economic returns for the industry with educational returns. Several philanthropists working in the space and interviewed for this study acknowledged this prevalent thinking while seeking ways to distance themselves from it. Proponents of the corporate model for digital education coalesced around the idea that democratic governance of public schools had failed and that schools and school governance must be reconceptualized under principles of the market. Harvard Business School professor Clayton Christensen linked the popularized concept of disruptive innovation to the business of online education:

> By 2019, 50 percent of all high school courses will be delivered online. This pattern of growth is characteristic of disruptive innovation—an innovation that transforms a sector characterized by products or services that are complicated, expensive, inaccessible,

and centralized into one with products and services that are simple, affordable, accessible, convenient and often customizable. Think personal computers, the iPod and MP3s, Southwest Airlines, and TurboTax. At the beginning of any disruptive innovation, the new technology takes root in areas of nonconsumption—where the alternative is nothing at all, so the simple new innovation is infinitely better. More users adopt it as the disruptive innovation predictably improves.[8]

Christensen's protégés, such as Michael Horn, used the idea of disruptive technologies as an explanation for how digital education will go viral and why it is better than traditional brick-and-mortar schooling. For Christensen and others, online courses and other digital education technologies will be high-quality products simply because they fill a void while claiming to offer affordability and accessibility. Horn asserts that "looming budget cuts and teacher shortages are an opportunity, not a threat"; they provide emergent markets in which modularized blended learning models based on high-accountability outputs reign over inputs.[9] Specifically, he recommends getting rid of conventions such as seat time, Carnegie credits, and student-teacher ratios, emphasizing that public school systems should eliminate many established rules of governance such as requiring that schools have record of student attendance or putting limits on the number of students a teacher can instruct at once. Much of what Horn offers is the well-worn choice and competition model. By making public policy around digital education closely aligned with market practices, schools will innovate in ways that make them work better for students and families. Students and families will in turn gravitate toward schools that are effective and ineffective schools will close. Everyone wins.

Clearly, Christensen, Horn, and others can offer important insights from a business perspective on what can create demand for digital education. But they are not educators in any sense of the word, and that shows. The narrative behind the idea of disruptive technology is that principles of the free market should be allowed to drive this surge, trampling, where necessary, public policies. The policies that they want to eliminate may be outdated bureaucratic practices created in an era focused more on standardization of instruction than differentiation. However, as we show in chapter 4, there are significant risks for eliminating these policies in the absence of careful scrutiny and proven alternatives that protect both teachers and students from abuses, such as overcrowded classrooms, whether they be virtual or brick-and-mortar.

Under the commercial banner, digital education isn't expected to just improve the quality of instruction. It also is expected to energize and create new education markets. One example is Startl, a not-for-profit supported by the John D. and Catherine T. MacArthur Foundation and the Bill & Melinda Gates Foundation, which defines its well-funded mission to "Shock the System": "We founded Startl to pave the way for cool new digital media learning products to move from an idea to funding and into learners' hands. We're working outside the established systems of public private partnership to break new ground in the education market and help launch the next generation of digital tools for learning."[10] For Startl and other disruption proponents, "to realize the promise of learner-centered education, we must create pathways by which sound, innovative, technology based products and services can evolve, mature, and get to market at lower cost."

From other proponents of disruptive education through digital education we hear that digital education will solve our work force problems and build our economy. In the words of Barry Shuler, former CEO of America Online, "Gone are the days of assembly-line education. The New Tech approach is exactly what increasingly competitive and global business leaders expect and demand in today's public schools."[11] However, much of what low-income students receive in digital education is highly standardized. Digital tutoring that is asynchronous (with no live teacher) and uses prepackaged curriculum as content for all students regardless of learning style is "assembly line education." And Jeb Bush, former governor of Florida, asserts that digital education is consistent with market models of education reform.[12] In a January 2013 op-ed for CNN, he wrote, "The right to a quality primary and secondary education is something that can and should be one of our most fundamental uniting American issues— and digital education is no exception. Thanks to technology, parents are empowered to choose not only the best school, but also the best course for their child."[13]

WHEN THERE ARE RULES, THEY ARE WEAK RULES

In this forward push of digital education, there is little in the way of substantive policy to monitor corporate involvement in education and/or to hold them accountable to the primary stakeholders in the public sector: students and their families. And when regulations on corporate work in public education are introduced, they tend to pose substantial problems.

First, policies regarding what for-profits can and cannot do in digital education can be ambiguous or unclear. Even before digital education, the state had a limited capacity to play a monitoring and effective regulating role, and these problems have grown with rising digital education enrollments. Consider the case of digital data. As demand for assessments and data grows, and as technologies are developed and sold for managing that data, the question of who owns the data becomes ever more complicated. When a state pays for assessment of student data in a charter school run by a for-profit management company, who owns the data? By asking who "owns" the data, we examine who has access to the data beyond basic FERPA rules, who sets restrictions on its use, who decides when and how data is made available to the public and in what form? Testing companies' use (and misuse) of data predates digital education. Recall the scandals in test score reporting and accuracy following NCLB. Now the responsibility for test score data has become even more significant and more muddied with federal mandates for computerized assessments creating lucrative contracts for multinational companies, like Pearson, that also have contracts to develop the tests used to compare the United States with other countries.

Second, government contracts may implicitly or explicitly override government policies when government capacity, such as time and staffing resources, to monitor them is weak. Consider this example. A parent sends her ninth grade daughter to an online charter school that is managed by a for-profit company. The parent thinks the mathematics curriculum is good but is shocked to learn that the English and science curricula are still being developed. The for-profit company has a contract with a for-profit vendor for curriculum. The contract between the two companies sets clear conditions for when either party might terminate the contract. This could include termination because the developer promised and didn't deliver a full curriculum. However, the for-profit charter company doesn't see this as cause for termination. Its CEO knows that when the curriculum is developed it will sell well, and the company has plans to buy the software company. The company's losses are not the same as those for the parent and student, who has her sights set on a four-year college. In principle, the charter school has bylaws that require that the curriculum be standards-based, but oversight of those rules has been weak because both states and districts are short-staffed. For the parent and the child (and the three hundred or so other ninth graders in the school), the "missing curriculum" carries enormous costs. Ninth grade is a critical year in college preparation, and a lost year is impossible to fully make up.

Third, limited information on digital vendors can pose problems for government oversight. It only takes a quick search of the web to see the ubiquity of the term *digital*. While states and districts hold contracts with vendors that require the companies to identify whether they provide digital services or online learning, or whatever term (*virtual, blended*) the state prefers, there are few clear guidelines or rules for establishing what *digital* means. *Digital* can mean everything from a fully synchronous learning program (where there is a live teacher working one-on-one with a student), to a netbook with the curriculum loaded onto it, to digitized textbooks. Because vendors have a lot of discretion in whether and how they self-identify as digital in these contracts, the information made available to the public, to parents or to teachers seeking new jobs with these vendors, can be deceiving and unreliable. What is called *digital instruction* by one vendor means something very different when used by another.

Furthermore, digital education companies have little incentive to do thorough self-examinations of whether products and services are of a high quality and are universally accessible.[14] Producing rigorous evidence of student outcomes (at the level we expect schools to produce) is expensive. Investors need to be convinced that these expenses will improve the bottom line rather than hurt it.

THE PROMISE OF EQUALITY

As in the case of contracting under NCLB, corporate models of accountability have been knitted loosely to the language of equality. From this perspective, when digital education disrupts face-to-face education, it can also disrupt the status quo. With this disruption structural barriers are magically dismantled, along with the disadvantages of learning differences, geographic isolation, and work and family demands. Digital education makes everyone equal, or, to quote Sol Khan, director of the Khan Academy, an online source of free math and science instruction, "equal before the evaluation": "Instead of handing out degrees, standardized assessments would be the measure of employee competence. Anyone could learn at their own pace in their own way: in an internship, as an entrepreneur, or at home on the Internet. Then, everyone, no matter how they were educated, would be equal before the evaluation."[15]

The undercurrent of these policy dialogues projects an appealing optimism about the potential of digital education to make substantive changes in children's basic access to education. It is hard to resist. We want schools to be better; we know that public education, not just in the United States but also globally, has underserved historically disadvantaged and culturally marginalized segments of society. Proponents of digital education such as the Innosight Institute, one of the leading proponents of blended learning, want us to believe that digital education can change that. Few parents would argue against a "movement that has the potential to transform America's education system by serving as the backbone of a system that offers more personalized learning approaches for all students."[16] Personalized education is responsive education—can digital education give us that?

The promise of equality in digital education frequently is framed in global terms, around global problems that are clearly urgent. According to the common message, digital education is not just a means of teaching; the technology itself provides a means of getting resources to people whose access to these services is blocked by the public bureaucratic pipeline. This is what business people and designers mean when they say, for example, that the problem of good digital games is a supply problem not a demand problem. The problem is how to get good digital games into schools without getting them clogged in bureaucracy. And it is what Catapult, for example, a digital not-for-profit funded by the Gates Foundation, intends in its mission statement: "Girls' and women's organizations are chronically underfunded, despite their key role in addressing inequality. One fifth of all women's organizations report the threat of closure, and two cents of every development dollar goes to adolescent girls." Catapult founder Maz Kessler describes the company as a "connector. It is a tool for people to take direct effective action to create change. Catapult unites online supporters with trusted organizations to help fuel the movement to end inequality for girls and women." Its projects include Mobile Literacy Class, which uses "mobile phones and texting to accelerate literacy for Afghan girls and children," among other education projects.[17] Harnessing the power of social networks, Catapult describes itself as a digital hub driving donations to organizations working to improve education. It is a good example of the expansive promise of digital education and equity-oriented proposition that drive much of this work. It is also an example of the multiple claims embedded in the notion of digital education as a means of equalizing resources. Catapult claims that digital education can reduce disparities in education by gender and asymmetries in financial resources.

These initiatives all sound very good and are greatly needed. However, it is important to recognize that every aspect of this discourse is about promises and potential, and there are for-profits and large not-for-profits that stand to benefit financially if we buy into those promises. And these promises are being made even when there is a good body of evidence which shows that market-based education reforms do not serve low-income students absent the right incentives and regulations. The public sector is held accountable for outcomes through test scores and high-stakes tests. Increasingly, every facet of a school's existence—from teacher performance, to school management, to content and design of curriculum and instruction—is organized around measurements by standardized tests. Meanwhile, companies selling educational goods and services, including digital education, to public schools are held to minimal criteria. The surge in education contracting has not been accompanied by anything in the way of meaningful standards of accountability for these companies.

When it comes to holding the private sector accountable, the assumption is that competition alone will work the magic. This is not surprising. The idea that corporations can govern themselves through by-laws and the larger market, even when they operate in the public sector, is consistent with the corporate (or contracting) paradigm. As one scholar put it, corporations are not only organized around the idea of contracts, but they are best described as "a complex web or nexus of contractual relationships. Every relationship that a corporation has with another organization is contractual in nature."[18] The implication from an economic perspective is that corporations can govern themselves and produce results, as "contracts inevitably generate outcomes that are ex ante efficient." From this perspective, the contract (and the competition) ensures that corporations and business organizations create the best product, innovate in ways that will meet diverse needs, and weed out inefficient or unethical vendors. This is exactly the assumption that digital education industry proponents such as Clayton Christenson and Michael Horne are making when they talk about disruptive innovations through digital education.

EARLY DEBATES

The problem is not that researchers haven't been paying attention to digital education.[19] Richard Clark argued more than thirty years ago that much of the rigorous empirical research and meta-analyses looking at the relationship between media and learning led to the same conclusion: media do not influence learning under any conditions. Where there are effects, he asserts, "it was not the medium that caused the change, but rather a curricular reform that accompanied the change."[20] Clark argues that technology cannot have direct effects on student learning without critical changes in both how and what teachers teach.[21] And the best current evidence supports the idea that media are mere vehicles that deliver instruction but do not influence student achievement any more than, to use Clark's analogy, the truck that delivers our groceries causes changes in nutrition. While our choice of vehicle might influence the cost or extent of distributing instruction, only the content of the vehicle can influence achievement. While research often shows a slight learning advantage for newer media over conventional instructional materials, this claimed advantage weakens in the face of compelling alternative explanations.[22] Others have taken issue with the argument that technology is merely a vehicle. Robert Kozma argues that Clark's delivery truck analogy is oversimplified.[23] He asserts that while technology may not directly influence student achievement, new technologies can act on the environment, changing learning settings and, by extension, student outcomes. Writing before the Internet boom, Kozma compares video disks to broadcast video, arguing that the latter offers students an expanded set of opportunities for searching for knowledge. He also argues that certain kinds of media allow students to perform learning tasks (searches and synthesis of knowledge) that they would be unable to perform without the media.[24]

Kozma's findings have been interpreted to suggest that rather than discounting the importance of media in learning or trying to lock down the question of whether new media as a whole help learning, we need more studies that compare different kinds of technology so we can see what kinds of digital media work better than others.[25] The idea that the value of CD-ROMs is different than the value of interactive digital curriculum with live tutors makes a lot of sense, particularly because our reference points for media have changed dramatically. We are living in the age of digital education, digital work, and digital socializing. Much of the research on the relationship between media and education since 2001 is based on the expected benefits of newer media: mobiles, digital games, and synchronous online learning. This leads some researchers to argue that the question between medium and content is no longer as relevant in the digital age, where technology is "not only providing new forms of content and connectivity but also assisting in transforming human roles and relationships."[26] However, even if some questions are no longer relevant, others are enduring. And, unfortunately, these are the very questions that aren't being addressed in current discourse around digital education.

UNCERTAIN EFFECTS BASED ON UNCERTAIN RESEARCH

People have high hopes for digital education. Policy makers, scholars, entrepreneurs, and educators view it as the conduit for improving the quality of public education. The virtual schools, online courses, gaming in the classroom, and tablets for every student that might characterize this newest wave of technology go way beyond simply having a computer in every classroom. Despite dramatic changes in the nature of the devices and the level of integration, this new wave is yet another chapter in an almost century-long belief in the transformative power of technology in schools.[27] But what is actually known about the impact of twenty-first-century digital education on the outcomes envisioned by its proponents? Scholars recognize the potential promise of new technologies for teaching and learning but at the same time caution against buying into the proposition that the simple introduction of technology improves teaching and learning.[28]

Indeed, the most consistent finding in existing studies of this new wave of technology integration is that we simply do not know enough about digital education to be conclusive about its benefits. Meta-analysis after meta-analysis has concluded that results are mixed, that the rigor of studies is uneven, and that there are big gaps in what we know. For example, in one meta-analysis of existing empirical research comparing the effects of traditional education and distance education on student achievement, attitude, and retention, researchers reported that in 232 reviewed studies of the effectiveness of online learning effect sizes were close to zero, with wide variability.[29] The authors' analysis thus suggests that some online schooling produces good results, while other programs perform poorly. Bernard and colleagues did find that when comparing the student achievement outcomes of synchronous distance learning, where the instructor and the students are online and progressing through the course together, and asynchronous distance learning, where the content is uploaded by the instructor and can be accessed by students individually and at any time, synchronous distance learning was not as effective as classroom instruction while asynchronous distance learning seemed to have more positive effects. Discussing their findings, Robert Bernard and colleagues admit that, due to scant research, they cannot offer any advice on how to design effective online learning experiences; however, they do suggest that opportunities for face-to-face interaction and collaboration may increase the effectiveness of online models. [30]

Research is beginning to point conclusively to the limits of using online instruction only, and people in the industry have started to acknowledge these limitations and now speak more in terms of blended learning or hybrid learning as the future of digital education, where the most promise and potential sit.

BLENDED LEARNING EFFECTIVENESS

Though much of the literature defines blended learning as a combination of online and face-to-face content delivery, there can be considerable differences in how material is actually delivered and how learning is divided between the two types of instruction. Various blended learning models include rotation, flex, self-blended, and enriched virtual.[31] We use *blended learning* to refer to any time a student learns at least in part at a supervised brick-and-mortar location away from home and at least in part through online delivery, with some element of student control over the time, place, and/or pace. Blended learning is seen as a way to marry the flexibility, access, and cost-effectiveness of online learning with the social aspects, individualization, and contextual benefits of face-to-face instruction.[32]

As is the case with distance learning, the research literature on blended learning models indicates mixed results. We looked for studies published since 2001 that have defensible designs and that focus on blended learning in K–12 settings.[33] Some studies suggest that blended learning models are more effective in improving student outcomes.[34] Others find that blended learning models have had a neutral or negative effect.[35] In general, there is a dearth of research on blended learning, and thus definite conclusions are difficult to make.

A meta-analysis of current empirical research on distance learning commissioned by the U.S. Department of Education found that blended learning is more effective than either traditional learning models or online learning alone.[36] Additionally, researchers found that learning is improved when students have control over their interaction with the online interface and when the interface prompts learner reflections.[37] The analysis of available literature showed that blended learning was more effective when the online component employed curriculum and instructional methods that differed from those used in the face-to-face learning component. And it also showed that blended learning is more effective when the online component is collaborative rather than independent. However, the researchers acknowledge that the available research on blended learning, especially in K–12 education, is scant. Further, the researchers admit that components such as collaboration and increased learning time may be the reason for the positive outcomes.[38]

What about the blended learning programs endorsed by the government and garnering much media attention? In 2002, the Education Development Center (EDC) evaluated the School of One pilot project to determine its effectiveness and examined the experiences of students and teachers during the implementation process.[39] Researchers gathered qualitative data through formal and informal interviews, thirty hours of observations, and course materials.[40] Overall, the students in the School of One program showed improvement. The mean percentage of items correct on the assessment, calculated by EDC, went up 28 percent. In other words, the data gathered by EDC via the students' assessment scores indicated that there was an average increase of 28 percent in the number of test items students answered correctly. In addition to the positive achievement results, the program was viewed favorably by teachers and students; all but one teacher believed that the program positively influenced student outcomes. Teachers also responded that the program could potentially help struggling students and students in need of individualized instruction. Around 80 percent of students gave positive feedback on the school's model. However, the study investigated the School of One summer math program, which mainly focused on reviewing material from the academic year, and the voluntarily enrolled students were already doing well in math.

In a 2012 study of School of One, the Research Alliance for New York City Schools investigated the schoolwide implementation of the program in three middle schools.[41] In the study the researchers utilized comparative interrupted times series analysis (CITS) to examine the unique effects of the School of One model in these schools. They compared School of One student achievement with that of previous students in the same schools before the program was implemented. Additionally, they compared School of One student achievement with that of students in other comparable New York City schools. The CITS analysis allowed the researchers to control for prior achievement and student demographics; it also accounted for city and statewide factors that may have had an impact on all schools. Researchers analyzed subgroups of students separately. Averaging results from positive effects at School A, neutral effects at School B, and negative effects at School C, the researchers found that School of One did not affect sixth graders' math achievement. But the impact across schools is statistically significant.

Developers of the School of One program postulated that student progress during the initial implementation might be impeded by a "gap dip," where students were filling in gaps in their knowledge instead of working on grade-level skills (the study did not measure growth on non-grade-level skills). In the exploratory analysis, students who were exposed to more grade-level skills grew more in terms of their achievement on the New York state math test. So far, there is no definitive evidence that this newest version of digital education, blended learning, contributes to improved student learning.

GAPS IN THE LITERATURE

There also are several troublesome gaps in the literature given the trends identified in chapter 1 and explored further in the cases that follow. First, there is a dearth of literature on the effects of online learning as it pertains to K–12 students.[42] This gap is particularly problematic given the explosion of online learning at this level and the considerable investment on the part of districts and private entities. Further, considerable policy attention at the K–12 level is focused on the academic benefits of online learning, with little attention given to the other kinds of nonacademic outcomes identified as important attributes of happy, successful individuals (e.g., social and emotional development, self-efficacy, school engagement). So while investor activity in online K–12 education is growing, research on online work at the K–12 level lags behind. Research on online or distance learning in higher education is much more prevalent and has a longer history, as online programs in that sector continue to grow.[43] The lack of research in K–12 online education is also problematic because K–12 settings have unique features that distinguish them from higher education settings (e.g., governance structures, grade level and content area objectives defined by policy, and the qualifications and role of teachers) and that create specific implementation challenges. Second, there is very limited research on whether and how online learning serves the needs of historically disadvantaged students, including special education students, low-income students, English language learners, and students of color.[44] This is especially pertinent since research indicates that these students are enrolling in these programs with different levels of frequency. In digital schools there are indicators of low-income students enrolling at lower rates, while in digital tutoring there are indicators of English language learners enrolling at higher rates, only to then drop out of the program. In addition, policy is moving in the direction of requiring more online learning experiences, which means that historically disadvantaged students will likely be offered the option or required to participate in online learning because those programs are expected to offer a cheaper alternative to traditional schooling.[45]

Further, online learning is being discussed as a way to personalize and differentiate instruction and to close skill gaps. This is often aimed at students who are behind and who have individual learning needs, which may include students from low-income areas, students of color, special education students, and other traditionally under-served students. For example, in the 2012 study of the School of One program, the researchers found that, on average, the model did not impact student achievement negatively or positively. And these results are complicated considering factors such as the gap dip and the fact that the analysis included some students who were not exposed to the School of One model for the entire year. Such studies are repre-sentative of the scant research identifying what works for students who are traditionally underserved as well as of the continued focus on deficit-minded skill gap frames rather than on the opportunity gap between resources provided in low-income and higher-income communities.

Third, there is limited research that can inform implementation of online learning. Some well-cited analyses and individual studies suggest that the variables that matter are whether educational tech-nology is implemented with fidelity and whether it is consistent with learning objectives. The problem is that this literature does not bring us much further than Richard Clark's basic argument from 1983. We know, for example, that "the single most important thing that research has shown is that what really matters is not the use of tech-nology but how it is used."[46] Robert Yegelski and Sarah Powley's 1996 work concludes that "even the most basic incorporation of technology into an educational setting can encounter technological, institutional, and theoretical boundaries.[47] From James Kulik and Chen-Lin Kulik's 1991 meta-analysis of 254 studies on the effectiveness of using com-puters to increase student achievement, we learn that both dosage and degree of support matter in terms of students' attitudes toward technology. The more students use technology and the more help that they get as they use it, the more positive their attitudes toward tech-nology.[48] But attitudes are not learning outcomes, and this and other meta-analyses are dated.

Existing meta-analyses are useful for pointing new research in general directions, but they tell us little about the relationship between technology use and other non-cognitive outcomes. Standard-ized tests are but one indicator of school performance. Other kinds of outcomes (e.g., collaborative skills, critical thinking skills, and skills of self-regulation and management) are conjoined with growth in academic performance.

Finally, there is very little implementation research that looks at how local and federal policy interacts with digital developments to shape opportunities for historically disadvantaged students. Where analyzed, policy tends to be treated as an isolated factor rather than an interlocking piece of whether and how digital education gains legitimacy in the face of limited evidence and under what conditions policies can be designed to support promising practices. This is problematic because online learning is (or should be linked to) part of a larger debate about how best to educate students in the context of dramatic economic and societal changes where the opportunity gap between the wealthy and poor is growing.

BARRIERS TO ACCESS BY FAMILY INCOME

Beneath the limited research on whether and how digital education improves student outcomes is a relatively ignored but critically important issue of central concern in public policy: equity. For-profit companies have immense commercial interests in the rise of digital education. The stakes also are high for low-income students. The economic gap between the wealthy and the poor has grown. The United States sits at the forefront of income inequality with 46 million Americans living below the poverty line. The United States also ranks low in terms of college-going rates, with just 25 percent attending college in 2010, far below anticipated work force needs. At the same time, the value of a college degree to individuals and the resultant social mobility remained high. Those graduating from high school earned less than half of what workers with a bachelor's degree or higher made.[49]

In public education policy, the primary beneficiary is supposed to be the student. The "typical" student in public education in the twenty-first century attends a city school, is living at or below the poverty line, is likely to be a person of color, and has a native language that is not English. Obviously, educating students and making good on the promise of education equal in quality to that of families with the means cannot be relegated to the contractual promises of the corporate paradigm. That commercial and at times government priorities make the needs of these students peripheral is reflected in growing evidence that students in poverty still face considerable barriers to accessing the services and products sold under the banner of digital education.

Specifically, while there are strong indicators of expanded use of technology for education in public schools, access to this technology is lower for students attending schools with a higher percentage of families living in poverty. In 2000, NCES reported differences in Internet access by school characteristics. This data suggests that in schools with high concentrations of poverty, only 39 percent of instructional rooms had Internet access, compared to 62–74 percent in schools with lower concentrations of poverty.

In addition, there is a significant difference in the rates at which technology access is increasing for schools with low and high concentrations of poverty. In 1999, the percentage of connected instructional rooms for schools with low concentrations of poverty increased 70 percent from the data reported in 1994; the percentage of connected instructional rooms in schools with 71 percent or more children in poverty was much smaller, only a 37 percent increase. Moreover, high-poverty schools also had a higher ratio of students to computers: sixteen students to one computer, versus seven students to one computer in schools with the lowest concentration of students in poverty.

By 2010, the NCES survey started to ask teachers how they used available technology. School poverty level continued to play a role, with teachers in high-poverty schools reporting less technology use for the following tasks:

- Used e-mail or listserv to send out group updates or information to parents: 39 percent of teachers in high-poverty schools did this sometimes or often, versus 69 percent of teachers in low-poverty schools
- Sent information to students: 17 percent versus 30 percent
- Used e-mail to address individual concerns with parents: 48 percent versus 92 percent

- Used e-mail to send concerns to students: 19 percent versus 38 percent.

Further, data from the 2010 report indicates differences in rates of usage of technology for instructional purposes between students in schools with high and low concentrations of poverty. Teachers in low-poverty schools were more likely to report students using education technology sometimes or often during classes to prepare written text (66 percent versus 56 percent) and present multimedia presentations (47 percent versus 36 percent), where teachers in high-poverty schools were more likely to have students use technology to learn or practice basic skills (61 percent in low-poverty schools, versus 83 percent in high-poverty settings).

In the Internet and American Life Project survey, teachers expressed concern about low-income students' access to technology. Fifty-four percent of these teachers reported that most of their students can access technology at school, but only 18 percent reported that their students have sufficient access to technology at home.[50] Similarly, teachers who teach low-income students are the least likely to say that students have adequate access to needed technology, either at school or at home. Further, teachers in urban areas are the least likely to report that their students have ample access to technology in school. Eighty-four percent of the surveyed teachers agreed that "today's digital technologies are leading to greater disparities between advantaged and disadvantaged schools and school districts," lending even more evidence for the existence of the digital divide.[51]

The more recent Pew survey reinforces these findings, showing that teachers' training in and use of digital tools vary depending on their students' socioeconomic status. For example, among teachers working in high-income areas, 70 percent reported that their school does a "good job" providing resources and support to teachers using technology in the classroom.[52] Only 50 percent of teachers in low-income areas reported the same level of resources and support. Similarly, 73 percent of teachers in high-income areas reported receiving training in the use of technology in the classroom, where only 60 percent of teachers of low-income students reported the same.

This disparity remains in the use of specific digital tools in the classroom. Teachers of low-income students report much less classroom use of tablet computers (37 percent) than their counterparts in high-income schools (56 percent). This same trend presents itself in classroom use of e-readers and smart phones. In fact, 56 percent of teachers in low-income areas report that students' lack of access to technology is a "major challenge" to using those tools in the classroom; only 21 percent of teachers in high-income areas report the same problem.[53]

There also appear to be access issues in online school programs that take the place of "regular" brick-and-mortar public schools. Students from lower socioeconomic backgrounds are enrolling in these programs, but for now their rates of enrollment appear to be lower than those for students from higher socioeconomic backgrounds.[54]

For instance, a study of K12 Inc. showed that its virtual schools enrolled slightly fewer low-income students than the U.S. average: 39.9 percent versus 45.4 percent.[55] Among total K–12 course enrollments, students from low-income families appear to be the least likely to participate in virtual or online courses.[56] Only 21 percent of students in online programs are considered low-income, which is much lower than the national average of 45 percent. The factors that may explain these differentials are likely to be differences in home access to the Internet.

There are differences by race, age, income, and educational level in whether students have adequate access to the Internet at home and *how* adults access the Internet. Among those who report owning smartphones, young adults, people of color, those not attending college, and those from low socioeconomic households use their phone as a main source of Internet access. African Americans, English-speaking Latinos, and whites are equally as likely to own a mobile phone. Income continues to matter in whether students under eighteen have access to high-speed broadband at home; 89 percent of students in families with household incomes of more than $75,000 per year have access versus 41 percent of students in families making less than $30,000 per year.[57] Much of digital education (digital schools, courses, and tutoring) assumes at-home access as a condition of full participation in courses. Data on home access to the Internet by income suggests this to be an erroneous assumption.

Given these findings, it is not surprising that students from lower socioeconomic backgrounds appear to be underrepresented in degree-granting K–12 online programs. As of 2011, 78 percent of students accessed online learning programs from home. Students also can access online courses at school.[58] However, families without Internet access may still enroll in distance education programs (e.g., basic dial-up), but they face considerable obstacles in terms of access to full course content once the school day ends.

Further complicating access issues is the rapidly changing nature of the technology and its requirements. A 2012 study by Common Sense Media, a digital media literacy advocacy organization, suggests that lower-income students have less access to educational apps. Low-income students, as compared to higher-income students, are less likely to have:

- A smartphone (27 versus 57 percent)
- A tablet device (2 versus 14 percent)
- Parents who have downloaded an app (14 versus 47 percent).

This means that low-income students do not have the same access to educational applications, many of which are free and a few of which have been shown to improve students' mastery in certain areas.[59]

Measures of technology access that assess whether a child has a mobile device (such as a phone) do not adequately capture the relationship between poverty and access to digital education. Students with basic phones can call their friends, but they lack the means and bandwidth to use mobile applications that help them do their homework, check their assignments, and prepare for tests.

CRITICAL QUESTIONS

In this chapter we argue that in spite of new accountability policies and industry trends promising better and wider access to student performance and other information, the dominant model of

accountability in the public education space is still very much a corporate model, one in which the marketplace is expected to regulate
itself via competition and where individual choice is seen as a proxy
for quality assurance. We also maintain that the claim that digital
education is an inherently superior alternative to other investments
ignores a certain reality: the vendors being paid to design and deliver
much of this schooling are corporations and business organizations
aimed at maximizing wealth of their organizations and shareholders.

Of course, we would never assert that corporations or business
organizations could be expected to prioritize differently, not with-
standing all the talk about social entrepreneurship. Nor are we
arguing that more policy and laws are the answer to addressing the
problems that emerge with any education reform, including digital education. Our point is that the corporate paradigm of accountability—
with its emphasis on the contract, self-regulation, and the concept of
externalities (that might include unequal access)—is an insufficient
model of accountability for digital education and other forms of education contracting, particularly in the absence of sound evidence that
digital education is a superior alternative to face-to-face learning and
in the presence of compelling evidence that there are clear disparities
in student access to these services relative to socioeconomic status.

Digital education may offer low-income students the potential
for greater access to curriculum and, when integrated with highly
effective teaching practices, more time for wrestling with ideas or
misunderstandings or learning in ways that are multimodal. Indeed,
some of the most influential proponents argue that the transformative
potential of digital education can be protected or isolated from the
interfering complications of economic inequalities in and across public schools. However, it is not clear to us how this can happen, particularly as essential issues are being ignored—equal distribution of
resources, democratic participation, and close alignment with public
purposes of public education. In these areas, digital education seems
to be moving very slowly, particularly relative to the pace and energy
of the commercial and policy imperatives.

PART TWO

Looking Downstream

CHAPTER 3

The Promises and Challenges of Instructor-Driven Digital Courses

ANTHONY, A SEVENTH GRADER, along with nineteen other students from his midwestern county, is enrolled in a blended course designed to develop students' leadership skills by taking on the identity of action researchers in their own schools. In the first week of class, the teacher posts the following question in an online discussion forum: "Do students have power in school? If yes—where and with whom? If no—how do students *get* power?" Students respond to the prompt, to one another, and to the teacher throughout the course of a week with specific examples from their own experiences. Meanwhile, they watch student-made videos of student action research projects in Oakland, California, that look at healthy eating choices in their neighborhoods. They also read a chapter from a print book on teenage leadership, specifically on the types of influence people can exert on groups, such as the charismatic influence of a religious leader or the coercive influence of a security officer. The following week Anthony travels to the local university to meet face-to-face with his classmates for four hours; there the teacher facilitates discussions and activities on the types of power students might have in a school, such as informal and formal, positive and negative. Then, over the next nine weeks, Anthony and his classmates conduct action research projects around a situation they believe needs to change in their schools. At the end of the quarter, students reconvene in person to present their findings through digital slideshows using Prezi, an online presentation program. Having chosen Anthony's topic of funding for early childhood programs as their final class project, the nineteen students together engage in a video production session where, over the course of sixty minutes, they write, practice, record, and edit a three-minute video on the topic, upload it to the Internet, and send it out to their friends, families, district superintendent, and state legislator to educate them on the issue.

This course is called "URule School: Leadership and Action," one of about ninety blended courses (both online and in person) offered through the Accelerated Blended Learning (ABL) program.[1] In this chapter, we draw on the participatory research of a team member who is also an ABL instructor to guide us through what it is like to design one of these innovative courses and to navigate the kinds of vendor-educator-policy dynamics that support the effort. Unlike studying traditional classrooms in brick-and-mortar schools, where researchers can walk into and experience the instructional setting, digital classrooms are much more difficult to "see"—unless you are a student or teacher. Participatory research allows us to get inside digital instructional settings in a way that more traditional research strategies may not.[2]

The ABL case shows the potential of digital education to use a constructivist curriculum that is both externally (in design) and internally (in practice) aligned to standards and driven by quality educators. It also illustrates the significant time, capacity, and communication this work demands. This is the kind of innovative digital education that should be readily accessible to low-income students in public schools. Instead, however, the digital education present in low-income settings tends to be "worksheets on a screen" or "drill and kill" work that demands little critical thinking or application of new concepts. Our look into ABL shows how digital education can be a vehicle for transformative curriculum: media is used to create a student-centered and educator-driven curriculum. This case study also

provides a powerful model in which students take on the role of cre-
ators, not just consumers, of media.

ABL is a not-for-profit, university-based organization that was
established in the 1990s to offer extended learning for gifted students. Gifted education coordinators and parents pursued funding
through regional foundations to create summer programs to, in part,
offset the services they felt the state's department of public instruction could not provide. ABL currently offers blended courses to middle school students across the state that mix asynchronous online
instruction with periodic face-to-face sessions during which teachers
and students interact in person. Students like Anthony attend public
schools that have signed agreements with ABL to make courses available, and then they enroll in courses through their school counselor,
gifted coordinator, or librarian. Each ABL course translates to a nine-
week quarter course credit for students and is designed to replace part
of a district's curriculum, typically in language arts. Students spend
their language arts class period working on the online portion of the
course, and three times a quarter students come together in a central location for four-hour sessions with their teacher and classmates.

The online portion of ABL's blended learning program uses an
open-source platform, or a virtual learning environment, to host its
courses. Groups of developers created open-source platforms such as
Moodle, Sakai, and Edmodo based on the principle of universal, free
access for users who could then redesign and distribute the platform.
Students and teachers use the online platform for asynchronous discussion, receiving and submitting reading and writing assignments,
and the assessment of student learning.

ABL enrolls approximately 1,400 participants per year from
around 130 different schools across the state. In the 2011–2012
school year, 13 percent (180 out of 1,384) of the participants were
eligible for free or reduced-price lunch. Compare this to the 2011–
2012 state demographics for school-aged children, where 42 percent
were eligible for free or reduced lunch. Approximately two-thirds of
students enrolled in ABL courses come from suburban areas, with
the remaining split evenly between urban and rural communities.[3]
The ABL program serves a largely middle- and upper-middle-class

population (87 percent), which is significantly higher than the state percentage of students from similar economic backgrounds (57 percent). There are numerous and complex issues related to this discrepancy. For one, ABL is subject to district identification of gifted students, a process that historically has been characterized by a racial and socioeconomic opportunity gap. ABL is engaged in the process of examining its program structure and strategy toward increasing the number of low-income students enrolled.

ABL AS A CASE OF DIGITAL EDUCATION CONTRACTING

ABL is situated within the market of digital education contracting because it contracts with schools for courses targeting a particular population—in ABL's case, gifted students. This type of contracting—instruction for specific populations—has a long history that includes contracts for special education services where third-party entities provide specialized staff (e.g., speech therapists or diagnostic assistance) to schools without the capacity to house their own staff members certified in these areas.[4] Similarly, high school students are increasingly turning to online Advanced Placement courses when their schools cannot support in-person classes, and many times this is funded by the school district.[5] These examples are consistent with the trend toward "unbundling" in educational contracting, where districts purchase a la carte instructional services (a course, a unit, or even a lesson) to address particular needs.

The level of oversight and interaction schools have with ABL is considerable and offers transparency. For example, the school-level coordinators have their own log-in access to the online course websites, where they can monitor student progress and teachers' assessments. They are in frequent contact with ABL teachers and administrative staff around both logistical (e.g., location of face-to-face meetings) and instructional (e.g., a student's lack of participation) issues. ABL also sends districts quarterly reports on student satisfaction surveys and learning goals and holds listening sessions to gather feedback from parents and school districts.

ABL produces all of its own course content and provides the instructors. The school contracts with ABL for one course at a time on an individual student basis. ABL signs an agreement with schools for these services, but the "product" is on an individual student level. This agreement is far less specific than those between districts and vendors in digital schooling or tutoring. It simply requires school-level staff to "release students from activities" as well as to "monitor student progress, make accommodations for online access, texts, transportation to face-to-face meetings, and assign official grades for the district." It also asks other stakeholders—namely, the students and parents—to sign the agreement. Districts and schools can enter and exit agreements with ABL on a quarter-to-quarter basis. Many school districts also become ABL "members" for $300 per year, giving them a discount on all course tuition, scholarship opportunities, and regular information and communication about courses. Membership does not obligate them to purchase courses.

Tuition is $195 per nine-week course for students in member districts and $250 for those in nonmember districts. Tuition for students eligible for free and reduced lunch is $25, supported by precollege grants through the state department of public instruction. Most schools pay the tuition through gifted education funding or special education funding. Since neither federal nor state law requires the use of certain amounts or sources of funding on gifted education, districts find funds for tuition from various corners of the general budget. Few schools ask parents to pay a portion of the ABL tuition.

Although ABL functions in a larger market of contracted services, it is also somewhat unique. The vendor is a small not-for-profit whose mandate did not derive from a policy mandate. It must remain sustainable and therefore make enough money to cover its costs, but it does not have shareholders to account for. Approximately 80 percent of the entire ABL budget comes from tuition (most of which comes from public school funding sources), and the remaining 20–30 percent comes from foundation grants and smaller gifts from families of ABL students.

ABL is an example of contracting for digital education, but why is it in a book about increasing accountability in digital education for low-income students when so few of its students are from low-income families? In essence, the other cases in this book illustrate digital education that offers access to low-income students but that is of mixed quality; the ABL case illustrates innovative digital instruction but limited access for low-income students. The ABL case offers a critical comparison in addressing the important tension between access and quality—how to bring transformative digital education to low-income settings.

DIGITAL CURRICULUM CREATED BY INSTRUCTORS

When you pop in your ear-buds and pump up the volume to your favorite tunes do you ever imagine yourself on stage? What is the musical journey from the songwriter's pen, to the stage, to the ears and hearts of the audience? Explore the many genres of American music, define your style, and start up a band! Step onto the bus as you and your crew of musicians discover what it takes to write music, find your voice, and go on tour! We will read classic poetry, ballads, lullabies and contemporary music side by side with non-fiction texts designed to help you become better poets and songwriters. We will play poetic techniques as our as instruments of expression when we compose our own songs. We'll discover why word choice, rhyme and rhythm all matter. Beyond songwriting, you will create a "Press Pack" showcasing your band both visually and musically. You will get a chance to sharpen your creative and informational writing skills as you book events, negotiate contracts, and pen music reviews. There is much work to be done when you *Step Backstage*.

This course description is from the syllabus for an ABL course entitled "Step Backstage." As with most ABL courses, the topic originated in student feedback about interest in future courses. The co-instructors developed the content using elements common to all ABL courses. Specifically, the entire ABL curriculum is organized into five "Modes of Engagement," or central ways of interpreting the world. All courses are situated within one of these five and therefore focus on skills (reading, writing, and interacting) necessary to develop the particular "professional identity" associated with each mode:

- The Human Experience Mode draws on the professional identity of a Historian
- The Identity Mode draws on the professional identity of a Reflective Leader
- The Systems Mode draws on the professional identity of an Engineer
- The Invention Mode draws on the professional identity of a Designer
- The Investigation Mode draws on the professional identity of a Researcher.

"Step Backstage" is located in the Invention Mode, where students are expected to grow skills toward benchmarks, such as "Write Like a Designer."

By design, all ABL curricula first focus on the student's interests in steering the content of the course and problem-solving activities and then teach or refine the skills needed to "solve" the central problem of the course. For example, the central problem for students in "Step Backstage" is to *sell* their band. The course focuses on creative and persuasive writing through reading and writing music reviews, writing song lyrics, and developing a press pack. All courses use the same template for the syllabus, and teachers must structure weekly modules in the online platform using the same four elements: guiding question, reading and research, concept development, and "show what you know."

The content is aligned to standards, but teachers create, revise, and deliver the entire curriculum. This is digital education without the textbook publisher or other vendor determining content. In other words, there are no subcontractors or content developers behind the screen, only the teachers who students meet and know. When asked about how she develops a new course, one instructor explained that she "backward maps," starting out by identifying the main goal or problem of the course, then the three main ideas that would support that goal, and finally the activities and resources that support those main ideas. For example, in "Step Backstage," the co-teachers brought together print materials (e.g., a book on how to write great song lyrics is required reading), online resources (e.g., students listen to music reviews from npr.org before writing their own review, read about and choose music genres using a wiki entry on American roots music, and use an online album cover creator for the soundtrack to their lives), and face-to-face activities (e.g., students read aloud a poem they have chosen to turn into lyrics using the print text). It takes a considerable amount of teacher capacity—both ability and time—to create and deliver curriculum such as this.

Curriculum alignment can be an important predictor of student achievement, and there are a number of strategies to assess the degree of curriculum alignment.[6] In general, curriculum alignment occurs when curriculum, instruction, and assessment share common structures, and in recent decades this common structure has come in the form of state (and now national) standards. *External alignment* is when a curriculum reflects the concepts and skills in standards and, ideally, the assessments. *Internal alignment* is when curriculum, instruction, and assessment reflect the "language and intent of the standards." In other words, the standards need to connect with actual learning experiences for students.[7]

Each ABL course identifies particular benchmarks, all of which are explicitly aligned to specific learning standards within the Common Core State Standards. A group of ABL instructors identifies those standards central to, as well as most relevant to, the needs of schools and the capacity of ABL. Based on this list, the group then develops and constantly refines the learning goals a instructor chooses in structuring a course. As one instructor explained, courses all focus on reading, writing, and interaction, partly because "that is the focus of Common Core; it's an overriding theme to our course structure." For example, the "Step Backstage" course lists three targeted learning goals along with the corresponding Common Core standards (R = reading, W = writing, or L = listening). For example, the "Read like a Designer" learning goal aligns with three different strands of the Common Core: reading informational text (RI), reading literature (RL), and reading for science and technical subjects (RST). This first number listed specifies the eighth grade level, and the second lists the standards within each strand to which the learning goal aligns (e.g., 8.1–8.9):

- Read like a Designer (RI 8.1–8.9, RL 8.1–8.9, RST 8.1–8.9)
- Write like a Designer (W 8.1–8.9, WHS 8.1–8.9, SL 8.5, L 8.1–8.6)
- Interact like a Designer (SL 8.1–8.4, SL. 8.6).

ABL courses are an example of both external and internal alignment to the Common Core. While alignment of course curriculum to standards can sometimes stop at the level of a provider application or a student's individualized learning plan—listing the standards upon which a course is based does not necessarily translate to alignment in instructional practice—with ABL the numbered rating (or grade) students receive as their assessment for the course is based on their growth specific to the learning goals, which are based on the Common Core State Standards. Students and instructors work closely with these learning goals throughout the course.

THE INSTRUCTIONAL STRATEGY

All ABL courses follow a common instructional format, blending an asynchronous online platform with three face-to-face meetings per quarter. Within the blended format, instructors are expected to incorporate course "designs that use a lot of game theory and integrated problems that become more and more complex throughout the course." Instruction based on game theory gives students frequent opportunities for making choices, in many ways dictating the direction of the course, and students are also presented with graduated levels of challenge as they move through the course. In the first week of the "Epic Failures" course for fifth and sixth graders, students receive the following assignment:

> This week, you will be placed into cooperative teams by completing a brief writing activity. The writing activity has two parts. First, you need to rank the following list of "wicked problems" in order

from most severe to least severe: racism, poverty, education, global climate change, disease, health insurance, war, technology, design of a new safe car, homelessness, political instability, cloning, famine, AIDS, communication, homeland security, crime, population growth, religion, money, and death. Second, you need to explain your reasons for how you ranked the wicked problems in a minimum half-page essay. This part must include how the following Law of Wicked Problems can help to explain your list order: "Solutions to wicked problems are not true or false, but better or worse." This essay is totally opinion based, but you will need to compare evidence to support your choices, and your response will determine which team you are on for the remainder of the course. Your finished essay will be added to your group's Design Journal once teams are formed and can be referenced throughout the course as you embark on the other challenges.

There also are lots of opportunities for teachers and students to interact, which, along with reading and writing, is one of the three central skills in the ABL curriculum. Facilitating constructive interaction in an online instructional environment between and among teachers and students can be difficult. In the case of digital tutoring, there are providers that purposely chose not to have live instructors run the course or to have any interaction between students. However, the director of the ABL explains the central role of online interaction in its courses: "The framework of the online interaction piece is something we can really build off of. The original online platform [for ABL] was a glorified chat board—we started with, 'How do we have great discussion with kids online?' That framed our whole approach to everything else."

These vendor decisions around the level of interaction between students and teachers matter to instruction. Research suggests that learning is improved when students have independence and an element of control over their interaction with the online interface, when the interface prompts learner reflections, when the online component utilizes curriculum and instructional methods that differ from those used in the face-to-face learning component, and when the online component is collaborative rather than independent.[8]

A central element to all ABL courses is the online forum, where instructors post prompts, readings, or videos followed with specific questions to which the students respond. Students are expected to respond to the original prompt as well as their classmates' comments. In fact, students only are graded on their responses to other students, not on their own original posts. The director noted that this puts greater emphasis on the interactions and prompts students to push one another. These forums are asynchronous in that students respond on their own time, not in a live discussion via a webinar or chat function. The forums are intended to be the classroom "discussion" for the online portion of the class.

The following is an excerpt from a forum discussion in a course for fifth and sixth graders called "Finding a Cure: Exploring the Amazon." The instructor posed the following questions on a Monday morning:

> What is your definition of progress? What does development cost? Should we sacrifice the needs of a few, for the wants of many? Should we sacrifice the wants of many, for the needs of a few? Before posting, visit this helpful resource [a link to a story on npr.org called "The Amazon Road: Paving Paradise for Progress"]! You can listen, watch, or read the story. You choose!
>
> When done considering the resources, answer this week's Guiding Question: Which is more costly: Progress or the status quo?

Jess responded to this original prompt on Tuesday at 9:00 a.m.:

> I personally think that progress is worst for the Amazon then status quo. Progress is paving roads and cutting trees. Status quo would mean the usual staying the same. As bad as it is now if they progress with the work it will be even worse. While progression is good for many it is also ruining the lifestyle, lands and beliefs of others. If something is to be sacrificed it should be the wants of the people who wish the roads and mining and dams. Everyone deserves an equal say. If one group decides it will be best for the roads to be built that is their say not another groups. The problem is that in order to save the beloved Amazon for the good of all the people both here and there. These sites have information and ways that you can

help in the fight for Amazonia [she then identifies four websites about saving the Amazon rainforests].

Then, at 11:50 a.m., Tyler responded to Jess's comments, pushing her for more clarity:

Jess, when I think of progress, I think of when I'm getting close to a goal I have. You sort of implied that it was anything that didn't change? Did you mean that? Or did you mean moving towards a goal that the people cutting down trees have?

That evening the teacher asked some follow-up questions of Tyler:

Tyler, you asked great clarifying questions of Jess. This would be a great opportunity for you to offer some insight into your thinking. Based on your definition of progress, do you see more good coming from progress than from staying the same?

Jess chimed in on Wednesday morning:

Tyler, I was not trying to say that progress meant staying the same. I said "Status quo would mean the usual, staying the same." For progress I mean that progress was the moving forward of the work, of the cutting of trees and deforestation.

Two days passed without any posts from students on this discussion thread, and on Friday afternoon the teacher interjected to get the discussion moving again:

Jess, thanks for clarifying your position. A perfect next step would be for you to ask a question in return. Has our conversation got you thinking or wondering about anything in particular? Did Tyler's question/reply give you any insight into his position? By asking a question, he can reply and our conversation can continue on.

Grace entered the conversation on Monday afternoon:

Jess, when I think status quo, I think mainstream. When you stick to the status quo, you do what everyone else is doing. I don't think it means stop doing everything and keep it that way. Trees are being cut down right now. If we stick to the status quo, they will keep cutting the trees down. They won't just stop and do nothing. What is your idea of progress besides roads and cutting trees?

The teacher then responded to Grace on Monday evening, pushing her for more:

> Grace, you make an interesting point about the definition of "status quo" and how it could refer to people sticking with the current plan or way of thinking. When I think of the word progress, I think of change and moving forward. Does progress have a positive or negative meaning to you? As a next step, consider sharing a specific example of deforestation as described in one of the resources. This would give your position even more creditability.

This online discussion around the question "Which is more costly—progress or the status quo?" continued over the course of the week and generated ninety-seven posts from twenty-four students and the teacher.

The decision to make interaction between teachers and students central to the ABL curriculum necessitated a particular type of platform that could host such interaction. Since ABL courses are designed to replace language arts courses, students access the online part of the class at all different times. This means that the course website platform must allow for asynchronous discussions, in this case the forums. These forums organize responses as discussion threads, graphically showing which responses are connected to which "parent" comment, allowing for simultaneous (but not "live") discussions around the same prompt. Learning in asynchronous discussion allows for prolonged conversations that give students time to reflect and respond multiple times, and hopefully at deeper levels. ABL students are expected to interact with one another, both in the online and face-to-face contexts, and are assessed on the quality of their responses. All forums in all ABL classes require students to post at least two responses to other students' comments, often with follow-up questions or their opinions backed with evidence.

The majority of ABL coursework is done online, which requires an Internet connection with enough bandwidth to play videos and work with interactive creative sites, such as Prezi. However, reliable Internet access is a major obstacle to bringing digital education to students from low-income families. While students enrolled in ABL rely on their schools to have high-speed Internet, many spend considerable time working on ABL coursework at home, which assumes that their families have high-speed Internet access.

From the existing research, we know that it is not enough to simply interject technology into an instructional design. It must become an interwoven and integral part of the instructional strategy in order to add value to learning opportunities and ultimately justify its use. In essence, we must ask, "Is the technology or Internet necessary for this particular learning to occur?" Besides the descriptions of course assignments, there are few elements of the ABL instructional design that could be effective or even possible outside of the online environment. Students from various geographic areas interact with teachers and students via the online website platform. As one instructor noted, "The ability to network with kids across the state in a bigger learning community, with like-minded kids, is a novelty." The online environment affords instructors and their students a greater opportunity to engage, as one indicated: "It's like having a one-to-one conversation with each student via online, whereas in a traditional classroom I may only be able to get to 2 to 3 kids in a class session." Another instructor remarked, "It gives every student a chance [to participate], but keeps all kids accountable."

Beyond facilitating greater communication among teachers and students, ABL courses leverage technology in a way that requires students to apply and develop higher-order thinking skills.[9] As opposed to simply using the Internet to deliver online textbook material, ABL uses the Internet to conduct research for projects and collect evidence for arguments in online discussions. The "Mystery Hunters" course provides a good illustration of how technology can be leveraged within a class to develop and apply critical thinking skills. Students in this course take on the persona of a time-traveling secret agent and work individually and in teams to collect information about historical figures in order to solve a mystery "problem." After working independently for the first two weeks, students see the following in the online course platform for Week Three:

Congratulations! You have proven yourself to be an asset for us and have earned a spot on one of our very selective special teams. Your mission will be shared with the group because the territory you are to cover is much wider. You will still need to work individually on some of the tasks because you never know when there is a mole in your group who might try to trip you up.

Task 1—Dossier: This is your first group mission. Your instructions are located in your group forum and the research should be divided equally in the group. Please follow all directions carefully, as it could be the difference between life and death. Most of the tools you will need are supplied but, as any agent knows, you need to be resourceful as well. That might mean talking to others, using information you learned in school or doing research on your own. Whenever you find information from a source that is not directly provided by me, please list that source (there are many counter-agents out there who are trying to foil your mission).

Students are divided into four "special teams," and each team is given different types of clues from the teacher to solve the problem. Asked "to be resourceful" in generating information, each team has its own dedicated online forum to discuss the clues from the teacher, information they find, and theories they have about the mystery. For example, Omega Group had the following discussion in an online forum:

Kevin (Thursday, 12:00 p.m.): Hey Omega Group, I think I know what one of the clues for week 4 means. The comic is explaining how Germany attacked neutral Belgium in World War 1. Britain joined the war because of that. However, I have no idea of what the random letters mean. Maybe a code? I will try to crack it, but if anybody knows what it means post it here. Go Omega Group!

Eric (Thursday, 1:05 p.m.): Its a cryptogram, like a code. Meaning we have to figure out the code in order to translate it.

Eric (Thursday, 1:45 p.m.): I did it! Coded letters: Qrjl vw yu zwky jc kpjyxwzqrcl. Decoded: laid me to rest in Switzerland.

Kevin (Friday, 11:30 a.m.): Good job Eric! You should be the official code cracker of the omega group!

Kevin (Friday, 11:45 a.m.): Aha! Doing some research I found that Wilhelm Gustloff, the head of the Nazi Party's Auslands orginization was assasinated in Switzerland in 1936!

Eric (Friday, 1:00 p.m.): And you my friend are the historical reference man!

Kevin (Monday, 8:00 p.m.): It was one of those things where you use picture and change some letters that it tells you to change, and i cracked it and it says lloyd gebner is my enemy! I googled him, but nothing came up. Maybe we can all research and we will eventually find something!

Rachel (Wednesday, 10:00 a.m.): It's not lloyd gebner, it's lloyd george. He was one of the main writers for the Treaty of Versailles. He is also from Britain. So, we can somewhat assume that the unsub is seeking revenge on him.

The ABL model comes from an instructional strategy rooted in constructivist pedagogy, where students learn through actively constructing meaning and knowledge. In the digital environment, it would be difficult to imagine a constructivist approach that did not involve live teachers or opportunities for students to actively engage with the Internet or one another. ABL's early decisions to make constructivist, interactive, game theory–based instructional strategies central to its program directed its later decisions about the online platform, blended format, and the role of the teacher.

In many cases, this type of innovative digital education is not what we see offered to low-income students. Instead, the scaled-up digital programs made available to tens of thousands of students in large urban districts are based simply in skill practice in the context of "worksheets on a screen." Students might progress through a series of close-ended questions to show "mastery." The differences between these formats and what ABL offers come down to critical decisions made by vendors about instructional strategy and format, which has a direct impact on the quality of learning opportunities offered students.

ASSESSMENT AND DATA USE FOR
KNOWLEDGE AND SKILL DEVELOPMENT

The ABL assessment system is based on the premise that the standardized and norm-referenced assessments in traditional learning environments fail to adequately evaluate growth relative to gifted students. Therefore, ABL developed "Pathways to Expertise," an assessment system that provides differentiated responses to student work and is designed to improve how students set goals for themselves. The responses target individualized, demonstrated needs and spell out pathways based on the Common Core standards, twenty-first-century skills, and, ultimately, expert-level goals. As ABL describes it, the idea of "expert learning goals" is based on equipping students with the research approaches, organizing tools, and theoretical frameworks used by expert communities (e.g., historians, researchers, etc.) so that they begin to view the world through this frame.

Specifically, the assessment is based on growth as measured by learning goals, which, in turn, are based on students working toward benchmarks that are directly aligned to the Common Core. Learning goals are created and revised by teacher groups, and teachers choose from the full list of possible learning goals based on particular student interest and need. Students submit their work, receive feedback from teachers, and choose whether to revise and submit the work again based on the feedback. For example, in the "Mystery Hunters" course, the teacher assigned the following during Week One:

> If you are accepted to proceed with this mission, you will be expected to blend in to different times and places. In order to do this properly, you need to be able to complete a site evaluation to gather information. Using the following sources (and any others you found on your own), complete the evaluation on Macedon in the year 336 B.C. Answer the following questions:
> - What is the native language?
> - What kind of currency is used?
> - How do people dress?
> - What is the religion?

The teacher then identified learning goals for each student in relation to this assignment, rated their responses to the assignment based on this learning goal, and provided written feedback. In the case of one student, the teacher assigned the following learning goal: "Discuss: Elaborate by adding more supporting details." Once she had read his response to the assignment, she rated it a "1," or "Novice," and included the following feedback:

> Good start but you need more information. Pretend you are talking to me about this information and I GUARANTEE that you would use more description than this. It is a waste of time to research and then never remember the information again. Make it meaningful— connect it to your life, make it interesting. For instance, can you tell me what this means IN YOUR OWN WORDS "The Macedonian native language is an indo european language"?

Both at the midterm and final phases of the ABL courses, students put together a portfolio of work that they have revised that includes annotated reflections on strengths and weaknesses of that work. The growth is measured and rated by teachers on a scale of 1–4, with 1 being "Novice," 2 "Apprentice," 3 "Artisan," and 4 "Professional." All of the ratings a student receives over the course of a quarter are combined into one final grade (0–4) and then translated by schools into the "local" grading system used by the district. In most cases this becomes the student's grade for their language arts class that quarter. Through frequent communication, feedback, self-reflection, self-assessment, and a structured revision processes, students and teachers co-construct the ABL assessment system. To a certain extent, they decide which data matter in figuring out how much a student has grown and in what areas.

ABL learning goals are used to assess individual student growth. The data used to assess student growth in a particular course are available to the student and teacher, with school-level coordinators able to access the course and grade book to check on student progress and parents able to access it through their student's log-in. Then aggregate data on learning goals and student feedback are used in reports back to teachers for their own course and professional development, so that, for example, they can set their annual instructional goals. Each ABL instructor receives a one-page summary report for every quarter they teach that includes data for the specific teacher compared to the average of all ABL teachers in areas related to both instructional goals and student satisfaction. On an aggregate level, data collected about enrollment, student pre- and post-surveys, and grades are frequently disseminated back to teachers and school-level partners. For example, twice a year ABL prepares a summary of such data and distributes it to all stakeholders.[10]

The assessment data available to ABL teachers, students, and school-level partners are in-depth and varied. It is intended to promote student growth but also program and course improvement. This raises the level of transparency for the schools that enroll their students, giving them a greater sense of how and where their students grow academically as a result of ABL.

The question remains, however, as to how well this constructivist and cooperative approach meshes with the reality of high-stakes standardized assessments in public schools. ABL can provide a numbered grade that schools can then translate into a course grade, but can we imagine going to scale with this system? What kind of time, money, and staff resources would it take for an entire school to adopt an online assessment system like this and to make it fit within the context of high-stakes testing? Going to scale is one of the central barriers to constructivist, instructor-driven digital education, and yet it is critical for reaching low-income students.

CRITICAL QUESTIONS

What Drives Digital Curriculum and Its Content?

The content is developed by ABL but is in no way a prepackaged program. In fact, it is responsive to the needs of the districts (challenging language arts development), it provides students expansive choice (among courses and within the course structure itself), and it can be quickly adapted to these needs because it is determined by the instructor. At its essence, the ABL curriculum is constructivist, highly interactive, and instructor driven. Teachers develop the content, appropriate it to the online website platform, deliver the content, and assess students as they interact with the curriculum. The instructors all work within a common set of expectations that the courses are aligned with the Common Core State Standards, twenty-first-century skills, and the idea of establishing expert learning goals—all central tenets of the program from the beginning. A constructivist curriculum, where the classroom is interactive and students create knowledge, would be very difficult without a live instructor who had the capacity to assess, adapt, and create learning opportunities for students as the course progressed.

This type of responsive, adaptable, individualized digital coursework requires highly trained and motivated instructors. All ABL instructors are state-certified teachers, and many have advanced degrees in the content areas or education-related fields, including educational technology. All instructors also must hold a state certificate in online teaching. Most ABL instructors have classroom teaching experience in traditional K–12 public schools. The director explained that they hire instructors partly based on their ability and experience in designing courses: "We are not buying curriculum. We define ourselves as a group of people who love to design curriculum. This unleashes great curriculum design and great teaching." Importantly, expectations for teachers to be curriculum developers is paired with frequent professional development and incentives to revise and improve the courses each year, as well as constant feedback from data analysis of surveys and from learning goals.

Figure I.1 helps us conceptualize how all of these characteristics—a constructivist curriculum and teacher-driven instruction and assessment—interact with each other to create a program model quite different than the others examined in this book. But the vendor's decision to use instructor-driven curriculum involves trade-offs. It takes considerable resources to rely on teachers to not only deliver but develop curriculum. It takes time not only to hire and train teachers but for the teachers themselves to create and refine curriculum. Time equates to money spent on professional development and planning opportunities. (For example, ABL teachers are expected to revise their courses yearly and are paid a stipend of $200 per course to do so.) And it requires constant communication on the part of teachers and ABL administration. These issues, as well as the constantly evolving nature of the ABL curriculum, also means that ABL faces great challenges if it ever wants to go to scale, expanding the districts it serves beyond the regional focus within one state.

What Drives Instruction and the Role of the Teacher in Digital Classrooms?

The online portion of ABL courses use an Internet-based, open-source program platform where there is a larger ABL host site, but other than this shell the course interface is completely built by the instructors. Both the instructor and students drive instruction, allowing for adaptability, variability, and individualized instruction on the part of teachers and self-directed learning on the part of the students. Teacher-driven instruction conceptualizes the digital teacher as more than a delivery mechanism or even instructor.

In the ABL course model, technology is not merely a delivery system. ABL students are required to use technology and the Internet in critical and creative ways to further their understanding of the skills they are learning. In a statement of her online philosophy, one instructor urged students to leverage "online resources to gain a better understanding."

Again, vendor decisions around the role of both the instructor and students in constructing the instructional experience affect the nature of learning opportunities. The ability of students to leverage the Internet toward learning is a critical part of the ABL model, but this presents important challenges for many schools and students. It requires a place where students can regularly access the Internet with enough bandwidth to play video and run development websites that are not blocked by oversensitive school Internet filters. And students need a strong foundation of tech-based skills to be able to navigate both the Internet and digital course platforms.

What Drives Data, and Who Has Access to the Data?

ABL collects data on just about everything that it does digitally. Data specific to the online platform (e.g., how much time a student spends logged into a course, the average rating a teacher gives for forum assignments, etc.) are collected through the open-source software program and can be downloaded into a spreadsheet format. ABL retains control over all of the data. Data on students, parents, and school-level coordinators' perspectives are collected through online surveys created, administered, and collected by ABL. It uses the data primarily for program improvement through staff professional development. The data are formative and lead to changes in course design as well as course offerings.

In addition, ABL uses data to report back to districts and schools about enrollment, participation, and satisfaction. The online open-source platform provides data on student log-in times and instructor activity. All feedback on assessments is provided in the course site, where both students and their school-level counselors can click on particular assignments and ratings to read teacher feedback. In many ways, teachers and students jointly create assessment data to map student progress. In the ABL context, data use goes beyond simple consumption to produce more knowledge for students and teachers and therefore is truly structured toward continuous improvement.

Again, there are important trade-offs in maintaining data systems such as this. It requires tremendous time on the part of administrative staff to collect, analyze, and present the data, as well as established avenues of communication between ABL and the schools it serves. Another important challenge to the collection of accurate and timely data is that ABL does not use or merge its own data with student-level data from the districts; any information on student demographics comes from the pre-course surveys students fill out. This has caused a particular problem in terms of an accurate accounting of students' racial and ethnic backgrounds. The exception to this is data on student eligibility for free or reduced-price lunch, since school-level coordinators identify these students based on their own access to district data in order to apply for the reduced tuition rates ABL offers low-income students.

This highlights the disparity between the amount of data collected between the online and the face-to-face portions of these blended courses. Much of this is due to the inherent nature of a digital platform that functions on systematized information input and records, and specific strategies for data collected on face-to-face sessions might involve observations using standardized instruments, which take time and human resources to administer. But the face-to-face settings are an equally important part of the instructional experience and also necessitate systematized and rigorous data for the sake of program improvement, in order to have a better sense of what actually occurs during face-to-face sessions, and to determine best practices.

This model of digital education is fully driven by teachers and is rooted in a constructivist approach to curriculum and instruction, where students learn through actively constructing meaning and knowledge. We see promise for digital education through examples such as ABL, but not without critical questions that foreshadow and loop through the other chapters central to this book. ABL offers the first of three cases examining the tension between access and quality—how to bring transformative digital education to low-income settings. Constructivist and teacher-driven digital instruction takes considerable resources such as time, great teacher capacity, and frequent communication between the vendor and end user. These demands may make it difficult for a small, regional, staff-heavy contractor like ABL to reach the scale of for-profit providers.

CHAPTER 4

Commercial Spaces and Opportunities to Learn in a Digital School

JUSTIN, A LATINO, is a freshman at Blended Academy (BA), located in a large, southwestern city.[1] He came from a middle school where the classrooms were too full, the facilities were dirty, and students were constantly getting into fights. He said he came to BA in order to work more with technology. After his first week, Justin said he enjoyed the school because he can work at his own pace; when he understands a lesson and others don't, he can move on. He wants to be a lawyer someday.

Two months into the year, the teachers bring up Justin at a staff meeting as an example of a student who just isn't getting the digital Pyramid curriculum. One staff member says that she watched Justin stare at the same Pyramid lesson for an hour, not understanding the content or passing the quiz. She describes that moment as "the definition of insanity," with Pyramid giving Justin the same material again and again and expecting a different outcome. She said that she instead sent him to Brain Game, an online learning tool, and sat down next to him to watch the instructional videos. Another staff member mentions that she had to get on Justin's case to set up a Google username, and another says that someone needs to get on Justin's case for hygiene, which has declined since he moved in with his transient father. Other teachers murmur their concern, but the conversation shifts away from Justin to Pyramid testing protocol.

Midyear, the lead teacher moves Justin from the mainstream Pyramid English curriculum into her separate reading class, which relies less directly on the digital content. Back in a more traditional English language arts setting, Justin earns a place on the school's honor roll. He is even invited to participate in the school's documentary project, led by a representative from a private educational technology company that the school board hired to piece together a video that could be used for recruitment. Justin ends up not participating, but the invitation speaks to his advisory teacher's belief that Justin has an important voice at BA. Toward the end of the year, Justin continues to have trouble with engagement in the digital curriculum for his nonreading classes, and the teacher takes his computer away from him when she believes he isn't using his time productively. When Justin is given a chance to get his computer back by completing a pencil-and-paper assignment, he declines. From our field notes it is unclear what Justin ended up doing for the rest of the day with no computer. A few weeks later his name appears on the suspension lists two days in a row for off-task behavior.

Justin is a student at a blended learning school: a public school that combines face-to-face learning with digital tools, such as online curriculum, toward the stated goal of providing more personalized learning or reducing the achievement gap. As Justin finishes his first year, news stories of the potential of blended learning proliferate. *Education Week*, the major newsweekly for education professionals, has built an extensive library of podcasts, webinars, and news stories that focus on blended learning; the Gates Foundation has hired RAND to conduct a study of blended learning schools. In June 2013 the first randomized control study of a blended learning math curriculum is released, showing positive effects, and it is heralded by some media as portending dramatic changes in math curriculum nationwide. Thought leaders in the business community, such as Clayton Christensen and Michael Horne, publish white papers that reimagine the future of public school through digital education, writing:

In the long term the disruptive models of blended learning are on a path to becoming good enough to entice mainstream students from the existing system into the disruptive one in secondary schools. They introduce new benefits, or value propositions, that focus on providing individualization, universal access and equity and productivity. Over time, as the disruptive models of blended learning improve, these new value propositions will be powerful enough to prevail over those of the traditional classroom.[2]

Much of the appeal of blended learning rests on the prospect of seamless integration of digital tools into the curriculum, as opposed to the more extreme displacement of regular schools by cyber schools. Many policy makers and academics are optimistic about the possibility of blended learning addressing some of the problems that have plagued schools—teacher shortages in high poverty settings, out-of-date expensive textbooks that appear to do more harm than good—by providing students, especially those with family demands or who are geographically isolated, with the flexibility to learn anytime anywhere.

The blended learning experiments that are popping up around the United States (iLearn, New York; Carpe Diem, Arizona) offer exciting learning potential. Evidence suggests that blending in, rather than using exclusively, online curriculum is the direction in which digital education in public schools should head. However, even with blended approaches, the contracted online curriculum exerts a powerful force on how teachers interact face-to-face with students and one another around content, instruction, and data.

This chapter explores a public charter school, managed by a not-for-profit organization, that contracts with a for-profit national developer of online curriculum as well as other vendors of software and hardware. This case of a blended learning school further reveals how, in the absence of strong or clear public policy, software vendors exert a powerful influence on the instructional setting: what students learn, the role of teachers, and the quality of data. Such a situation creates opportunities for vendors, who might otherwise be seen as marginal or technical players in school reform processes, to have influence on critical public policy issues, such as equal opportunities to learn within the school, the health and well-being of students within the school, and efficient use of public funds.

DIGITAL SCHOOLS

Rather than a set of courses, the experiment in digital education we examine here, Blended Academy, is a public charter school whose mission is to increase students' sense of school connectedness and their opportunities to learn through a face-to-face blended program of digital college preparatory courses, projects, and community service supported by integrated social and academic services. BA is a self-sustaining school community with a student body, full-time teachers, counselors, a principal, social workers, remediation specialists, English language teachers, project teachers, and learning coaches. This blended school is organized around the principle of high touch–high interaction learning plans. The school has an actual physical home—a building space—as well as a virtual home that is open 12 hours a day, 7 days a week, 365 days a year.

The theory of action on which BA is based begins with the consideration of a number of variables in school organization that can be manipulated: scale, time, and place of operation; staffing; information and communication systems; and school, family, and community relations and interactions. By reimagining schooling along these axes, an entirely new form of high school could be created. The primary outcomes the program targets are: for the student, college and career readiness and action, twenty-first-century skills, physical and mental health, and civic engagement; and, for the future of the school as a model alternative, credibility, reliability, scalability, and sustainability.

BA leaders and designers specifically intended the school to be a digital alternative to full-time, fully online virtual schools. From their perspective, blended learning should not be confused with online learning, whereby teaching and learning occur primarily via technology with students and teachers infrequently or never meeting face-to-face (e.g., Florida Virtual School and K12 Inc.). This other class of blended learning assumes that learning can be effectively mediated by technology and minimizes the importance of face-to-face interaction.

Instead, the theory of blended learning behind BA's approach is much more complex and multilayered. The program blends high access to differentiated learning opportunities (digital courses, projects, community service, and dual-credit courses) with support frameworks anchored in face-to-face interaction and comprehensive student support to promote student engagement. It also blends high levels of access to "the best of technology" in data analytics, mobile devices (laptops, iPods, and iPod Touches), and digital curriculum with the smart use of data as the means to achieve highly personalized learning plans and customizable individual schedules. The system provides teachers, administrators, parents/guardians, and students with regular, up-to-date, and actionable data about student performance and progress.

Blended Academy differs from ABL courses in that it was designed primarily to serve low-income students identified as academically at-risk. Approximately 75 percent of its first-year population was Hispanic, approximately 30 percent were black, and less than 5 percent were white. (The teaching staff was also racially diverse, reflecting the composition of the student population.) And 80 percent of its first-year students were eligible for free or reduced lunch. BA draws on federal and state subsidies targeting low-income students to fund its program. Most students reported in a first-year survey that they rarely had access to a computer, mobile device, or the Internet at home. For these students, the digital school is the primary setting through which they can access digital curriculum. The majority of students reported that the content and character of the digital schools, particularly the role of teachers, was very different from what they experienced in middle school.

At its inception, the program's vision of instruction was to provide social and emotional supports to students as a key aspect of the school experience, in keeping with the common understanding that these supports are critical to high-performing low-income schools.[3] In this regard, Blended Academy is a school designed around the expected instructional needs of low-income students. However, the curriculum it initially purchased was not designed by teachers but was a commercial curriculum owned by a for-profit content provider.

BA AS A CASE OF CONTRACTING FOR DIGITAL EDUCATION

While in rare instances public schools may be able to make the software needed to create a blended program on their own, the complexity of blended learning places time and resource demands on schools that can make leasing curriculum, data, and instructional services from software providers seem a better alternative than building them in-house.

The operation of the digital school involves multiple layered contracts, with different kinds of government agencies involved in the purchase of aspects of the digital schools. KIPP is a not-for-profit charter management organization that operates both digital and non-digital charter schools by contract with districts throughout the country; its Empower Academy is a not-for-profit charter school with its own governing board and set of bylaws. Rocketship is a not-for-profit charter management organization that has a management contract with San Jose to operate charter schools. It also has its own governing board and, as in the case of KIPP and other schools, may have waivers from some state regulations, though it is responsible, as any regular public school is, for complying with other mandates, like federal special education laws and state and federal requirements for standardized testing.

Digital schools contract with one or more outside vendors for multiple kinds of services (both instructional and noninstructional). There are contracts for managing student information systems and blending them with academic data; there are contracts for digital content to supplement and work alongside units teachers develop in class; there are contracts for online teachers in the form of videos and tutorials intended to make more meaningful use of teachers' time. These contracts are supported with public funds combined with private philanthropic money and investment dollars. The contracts

also are legitimated through government endorsements or sponsor-
ships, as in the case of the New York City Department of Education
iZone schools. The contracts are being developed in the context of
large charter school networks, such as KIPP and Rocketship, and are
creating the potential for vendors to more rapidly scale-up revenue
and gain resources from the government in order to fuel the sale of
the product.

Take the example of a fictitious school enrolling 125 students
with an average daily attendance of 110. In this school, public revenue approaches $1.5 million annually. Approximately $24,000 of
those funds is returned to the charter school management organization or district as part of a governance fee. Other digital schooling
costs include the lease or purchase of software, computing personal
devices, other hardware, software/platforms, and digital content.
There are additional contracts bundled into software/platform costs.
For example, a blended learning school typically might contract with
industry leaders such as Blackboard for learning management systems. It could have single or multiple contracts with companies such
as Powerschool from Pearson or Discovery Software from Tyler Technologies for student information systems. It might also pay regional
centers such as the Southeast Regional Evaluation Center or for-
profit companies such as Discovery Software for software and support around formative assessment and still other vendors, such as
ERP, to handle payroll finance and inventory. And there may be additional contracts for content providers. Discovery Streaming, Promet-
hean, Apple, and Android, for example, might be paid for curricular
content in the form of e-books, streaming content, and apps. In digital schools, hardware and software (e.g., Apple computers and Micro-
soft Office user fees) are leased for an annual fee and frequently on a
long-term basis (e.g., six-year contract).

Contracts for software and hardware are a critical component of
blended learning charter schools. They bind the material and technological inputs of digital schooling to the larger public policy frameworks that legitimate and fund the purchase and lease of services
and products. However, when a charter school contracts with a private company, the details on what hardware and software data has

been purchased or leased is not easily obtained. The contract frequently specifies that specific information on the terms of the sale is not to be made public. In these contracts the financial costs of digital schooling become more transparent. There are break-out costs for each course per student per year, and the fine print may specify that this does not include any course materials. There are budget lines for professional services but none for books. Digital school contracts typically contain a paragraph or two that seem not to be related to teaching and learning, where they talk about user support: who to call/e-mail if there are problems with the technology. The user support is identified as a built-in feature of the curriculum provided at no extra cost; however, the contract, which reflects the interests of the primary parties in the contract (the software vendor and not-for-profit managing the school) and focuses primarily on reducing costs, makes no mention of the hidden costs or benefits born by or afforded to teachers or students when instructional issues with the software or hardware arise, such as when a student can't access a course or when grade book data is not available.

BLENDED ACADEMY

BA is housed in a large office building attached to a hotel. Depending on which way you enter BA, you may be on a largely empty street, pass professionals going about their daily routine, or find yourself among a transient community of hotel guests. It is a difficult location to find for someone unfamiliar with the area, and the surrounding community provides no indication that you are in the right place. On learning that Blended Academy was located across the street from his office, one local businessman said, "I always wondered what went on in that building. It just seemed like vacant offices."

Most students come to BA after a long journey on public transportation involving several transfers. Sometimes travel time can be over an hour, as each train or bus makes numerous stops in the congested city center. The buses and trains are crowded with people, and often there is only room to stand. The nearest subway station is eight long blocks away, and few buses stop directly in front of the building.

Parking in the area costs anywhere from $24 to $36 a day, so many teachers also take public transit.

Within the building, several security stations dot the main corridor, where guards watch as people roam the empty hallway. The ceilings are high, and everything is hushed and muted. When there are people in the corridors, they speak in low voices; anything louder is apt to echo throughout the building. Occasionally, people emerge from the elevators connecting the building to the parking garage, but none lingers in the corridors for long.

But on entering the school doors, everything changes. Between class periods the hallways are crowded with students, and teachers stand in their doorways offering greetings, jokes, or admonitions. As they roam the hallways, students talk loudly and listen to their iPods. Bulletin boards line the wall. Some have pictures of students and teachers, administrators, and staff; others feature student work or serve as a place of recognition for exemplary students; still others contain notices for club meetings or flyers.

Locating the school within a commercial building was intentional. BA's founders did not want a traditional school building with small classrooms, blackboards, and few electric outlets. They wanted a space that could support a range of technology, a space where they could tear down walls to create room for a rotational model in which students could move through different kinds of activities, like individual work on the computer, group work, and project-based work.

INADEQUATE DATA IN A HIGH-TECH ENVIRONMENT

As envisioned by schools leaders, and consistent with the blended learning ethos, the digital curriculum, while supplanting the textbook, was not intended to supplant the teacher. Instead, the role of the teacher is flipped: basic content is delivered via the online curriculum, and the teacher is expected to enable and support students' mastery of content through "live" supplementary activities targeting the concepts or skills individual students may be struggling with. However, the teacher's ability to assume this role turns on a number of conditions: access to relevant data, the quality of data, and teachers' capacity to make sense of the data in ways that inform their instruction. The model that BA has articulated and begun to deploy attempts to address some of these conditions. The vision was to blend the digital curriculum with a new style of teaching, one in which the teacher assumes the role of guide/facilitator/mentor and moves away from pedagogical models involving lecture-based front-of-the-room instruction. But BA found that without a directly aligned data system, the administrative burden of attempting to manage an entire school population around a personalized academic problem was impossible.

While the school hired a full time instructional specialist to help build these systems to address issues of attendance, discipline, report cards, and parental contact, the majority of this specialist's time has been spent solving low-level technology deployment issues. She installed a camera system in the hallway when serious discipline issues mounted, troubleshot when students could not get access to the curriculum, and figured out ways to restrict access to pornographic material for teens in a school culture built on a vision of open access. But when not dealing with the daily operational efforts of supporting technology deployment, she has focused on identifying the appropriate mechanism for data collection and presentation with the goal of automation, so that time will not be spent on generating data but, instead, on interpreting data and using it to develop appropriate and personalized instruction. From the perspectives of BA's founder and the technology director, this kind of system, rather than the Pyramid curriculum, is the most important and the least understood aspect of blended learning. Board excitement around the data systems, which a contractor was developing for the school, mounted. In a December meeting, the founder remarked that beyond helping Blended Academy, "there is a demand for these systems in the K–12 market. Schools that have an online component need systems to feed data on students' progress in the online curriculum back to teachers."

But before data can be useful for teachers, it needs to be good data. It needs to be valid, it needs to be relevant for teachers in improving their instructional practice, and it needs to be available (both in terms of timing and format) to teachers in ways that enable its use. And most of these conditions were not met during BA's first year. There was considerable technology in place and the promise of better data throughout the year. Pyramid, the curriculum purchased by BA, compiled student scores on computer-scored tasks, which automatically transferred into a grade book that the teacher and administrators could view for each course and that was linked to a default course calendar for each student, with class ranking designations for each student automatically calculated. However, in the interim, teachers struggled in the face of vendor's control over data that seemed to make good, personalized teaching more difficult. The biggest problems they had were not being able to synthesize data, like running class reports, and not having that data tied to attendance, discipline, or parental contact.

From one staff member's perspective, the data coming out of the online curriculum was "ridiculously insufficient and hard to mine," requiring "twenty clicks to access student-level, classroom-level, or teacher-level data." In a school that aimed to reduce the opportunity gap, the interface did not allow school administrators to disaggregate data or pull out data on academic progress and match it against demographic data. One teacher said, "So I can't see how my African American kids are doing, how my English Learners are doing." For example, a teacher who wants to understand why a student was forty-five assignments behind in the online curriculum, and then determine whether it might be associated with the student's attendance, would hit a digital wall. And when a teacher downloaded his online grade book, a summative unit score would pop up on the screen. And there was no report that could separate out how far behind the student was in a particular class; with most high school students having at least four different classes, the teacher had to run separate lists, export them into Excel, and sort them.

Furthermore, the data being generated wasn't reliable data. Two indicators used to assess students' mastery and progress were not valid. The first was the status indicator. Students were identified as red, yellow, or green based on the number of units completed in the course (red being the fewest and green the most). However, the status indicator was not reliable. Students identified as withdrawing from the program were also identified as having "mastered content in a course area," and students identified as completing the course were also identified as red in terms of their course progression. In addition, students could ask teachers to adjust assessment due dates in their digital curriculum calendar, which could change their status from red to green. While many students took the initiative to ask for these extensions, those who didn't were left as red even though they might have completed the same level of mastery as another student.

Second, the withdrawal data was used as catchall for any number of actions by the student and provided little clarity on the rationale for why a student withdrew from a course, information that is needed for designing an appropriate intervention. The student might be identified as withdrawn because she dropped the course, was enrolled in another course, or left the program altogether. Further, students could be withdrawn because they mistakenly enrolled in the wrong course, were moved to a course with more language scaffolding, or left the school.[4]

The Pyramid system was promoted to teachers as enabling them to personalize learning in ways not possible in regular public school classrooms. In reality, teachers found that the data generated by the technology told them very little. This problem was particularly acute around the Common Core State Standards and twenty-first-century skills to which the curriculum was purportedly aligned and the school and state were committed to achieving. In the words of one teacher, the computer could not "handle writing and comprehension assessments." If a student had completed all of the assignments, the completion of the assignment would not be reflected in the computerized grade book, and the teacher would need to go in and add that grade manually. The computer also couldn't handle partially completed writing assignments or writing assignments still in draft form. In this scenario, the teacher would end up entering place-marker grades, "putting in like 79 percent for students who had turned something in but hadn't been graded yet."

However unreliable it was, the available data was used by administrators and staff in performance evaluations of both students and teachers. In focus groups, students reported that their placement in the red or green column was used as a basis for disciplinary sanctions or for special recognition; if consistently in the red, the school took away students' tablets and other technology as a penalty, whereas students in the green were identified as leaders. In interviews, staff members identified the use of Pyramid completion data in the ranking of students and teachers as contradictory to the vision and mission of the school. Teachers who worked after hours with students one-on-one, who sought to connect students with resources linked to interests, and who worked on authentic multidisciplinary projects also tended to be the teachers with high percentages of students identified as in need of improvement. Interestingly, while these measures were used to evaluate teachers and students, the school did not issue any report cards until the end of the year. The school's new computerized assessment system didn't have the recorded data that it needed. This made the generation of report cards more time consuming, and much of it was done manually.

Paradoxically, in the high-tech environment of BA, teachers often reverted to low-tech strategies because of the failure of the digital curriculum and data to hold students accountable and to see how much progress they were making. This included writing notes on Post-Its and putting them on students' computers to remind them on what lesson they were to be working. Teachers' strategies also included verbal rather than digital management of student work. For example, one teacher explained her process for keeping students accountable:

> I call their name, but when I call their name, they don't say here. They tell me what page they're working on . . . I'll call their names, take role, and then check what page they're on. While I'm doing all of that, students will sign in, and if they need something, if they need a test unlocked, if they need me to review a quiz with them, if they don't understand a particular activity. They'll sign in, so by the time I get all of this going, I have a list of students. I can sit down and then go through the list. I try to make it where I go through three students, and then I stand up and then go and check

on everyone else because I know proximity is important and I don't want the class to get out of hand. But normally, because on the board I have exactly what should be done every day, and where they should be every day, then they understand, like, oh, by today, I had to complete the [test] for Unit 1.

Teachers also relied heavily on nondigital strategies for keeping the students organized. One teacher had students create their own notebooks so that they could organize themselves and have a study guide. She supported this practice by saying:

I think that organization is a big thing, and structure. I know that gluing things in a notebook may seem very childish to some people. I did it when I taught 10th and 11th grade. And it was fine. And it's just, just for them, it's like, I tell them, this notebook, this is like you creating a book. At the end of the semester, you can go back and look at everything you've done. Plus, when you take your final exam, you don't have to go into Pyramid, or the textbook (that's our textbook), and look for all these things, they're already going to be in your notebook. So it's a resource that you will continue to use.

Although this teacher used Pyramid in her classroom consistently, she did not want students to rely on it as their study guide. She confided that she wanted to utilize the digital curriculum and was determined to eventually enact the blended model as envisioned; however, she felt that the structure was not in place to allow teachers to cater to individual student needs or to keep students progressing through the curriculum and mastering the content. The tension between wanting to enact the model as intended and not having the necessary experience or resources to do so compelled this teacher to constantly redefine her role and to rely more on traditional strategies than she would have liked.

Student experiences varied from class to class; they were held accountable in a variety of ways and to various degrees. Some teachers focused on progress through the curriculum to hold students accountable. For example, teachers set goals for the week and stipulated where students needed to be by Friday. Other teachers stated class goals for the day. Still others encouraged student progress by mandating that anyone who was behind had to stay after school to finish their work. Teachers struggled with how to measure progress; some resorted to counting the minutes students were logged onto the system. Consistently checking in with students to see how long they were spending on courses and how quickly they were progressing became one of the teachers' main tasks.

Other teachers attempted to develop students' accountability to themselves and their classmates in other ways. For instance, one teacher often made explicit attempts to give his students more power by telling them that they could choose whether or not to be on task but that they had to respect other students' decisions to work. In one exchange, this teacher attempted to redirect a student by appealing to her sense of responsibility to others, saying, "If you're going to be off task, please don't bring other people with you." This strategy worked to some degree with some students, but not many.

Teachers recognized that progress did not necessarily mean mastery in the Pyramid curriculum. So getting students to master the content became another layer of responsibility for the teachers and the students. Some teachers conducted oral quizzes in groups to assess students themselves and to reinforce Pyramid material. Others sat with students and worked through quizzes individually, requiring students to talk through how they got their answers and what their thought process was. Teachers also developed in-class processes that deviated from the curriculum in order to make sure students were accessing and understanding the material.

IMPLICATIONS FOR SCHOOL CONNECTEDNESS

As teachers and staff at Blended Academy navigated the lack of adequate data systems and the ambiguity of teachers' roles within a new blended environment, the school program lost key components of its theory of action. BA was designed to increase students' opportunities to learn and improve school connectedness. It was to increase opportunities to learn through providing extended hours and online-, project-, and community-based learning and by offering high teacher quality in the form of online master teachers, highly qualified on-site staff, and teaching assistants to support student learning. Improved school connectedness meant highly personalized learning plans through scaffolded content support provided by virtual master teachers within Pyramid, individual and group projects, and internships and a comprehensive "system of care" that would provide social services to students and their families And as the school staff was hired and plans for implementation began, the plans for school connectedness were expanded to include an advisory program focused on social-emotional learning, a school culture centered around student leadership, and extensive community partnerships that would provide students with services and function as sites for students' own community service.

But in practice, during BA's first year of implementation, the school lost key learning opportunities and nearly all initiatives designed to foster school connectedness. Advisory time morphed into a check-in time for student progress on Pyramid, and explicit social-emotional learning happened exclusively in disciplinary sessions. Similarly, student projects took two forms: Pyramid-related projects that teachers developed as alternative assessments and disconnected workshops led by community artists or other partnerships. These projects occurred sporadically throughout the year and, with the workshops, were often limited to just those students who had made sufficient progress in Pyramid. Still, teachers continued to express a desire for the space and time to incorporate projects: "How can I, in this structure, implement labs? Do projects? So we can, you know, not just have students sitting on the computer doing Pyramid all day."

THE NATURE OF THE DIALOGUE, OR LACK THEREOF

Why did Pyramid grow to be the school's focus rather than project-based learning or social-emotional learning? While we cannot point to one definite answer to this question, we do have some sense that a lack of sufficient and reliable data systems contributed to the loss of school connectedness in BA's implementation. With the teachers and staff having put in significant time to establish critical school processes like discipline and teacher evaluation, there was little time left for other program development. By mid-November, for example, the administrator responsible for social-emotional learning stopped sending out advisory lesson plans: "We really couldn't focus on advisory because everybody was overwhelmed with Pyramid . . . That's no longer my role, my focus right now . . . Because I had to become everything else . . . So advisory kind of became a 'you need to kind of put that on the back burner right now, we need to focus on this' kind of thing."

We found that the governance dynamics at Blended Academy complicated the school's ability to address its needs. Decisions often came in the form of top-down solutions to market-generated problems that trumped the ground-level problems faced by students and teachers. Those responses also complicated the school's vision of expanded access to learning. From the start, the school's design reflected a corporate imagining of the school space; the proposal called for "a place in which students feel at home, productive, and proud" and yet boasted the affordability of the school site in "underutilized and inexpensive commercial space." The school's design and charter also identified students from high-poverty areas as its targeted population, and throughout its development the school's leaders received inquiries from interested families about whether the school would be located in the high-poverty areas from which the school was trying to recruit. But based on market issues of affordability for the school space, a downtown selection took precedence over accessibility, which created ongoing problems with recruitment as families in higher-poverty areas did not want their children making the commute.

Founders and leaders' decisions often seemed to teachers to be at odds with the public mission of the school. Money was spent on hiring an instructional specialist, who was paid more for four months of consulting work than some teachers made in the whole year. Issues that would have been considered high priorities in a public district or school governance agendas were, in the climate of contracting and technology, considered no big deal. For example, by the end of the school year, there was no teacher evaluation plan; decisions concerning teacher evaluation were not considered policy decisions. Instead, very critical decisions that bore directly on the quality of education were considered small-scale actions that, within BA's governance structure, could be dealt with in a number of days.

The top-down problem is common in all kinds of schools, blended or not, so what makes this a problem particular to digital school contracting? Partly it is because it shines specific light onto the nature of dialogue—or lack thereof—between contactors and schools and then between school administrators and teachers. It also shows that the promises of systems innovation on the part of contractors can easily fall victim to the same "do as we have always done" habit for which regular public schools are criticized.

And while the actions of individual teachers who mobilized and worked to make good on BA's vision were important, they did not (at least in the first year) seem to play as crucial a role in students' overall aggregate experience of blended learning. Absent teacher input, the software had a deliberate and negative impact on teachers' ability to make informed and evidence-based instructional decisions. Teachers held students accountable to the tasks set by the curriculum provider, and administrators informally held teachers accountable for the students' progress within the curriculum. Also, the curriculum came to assume an importance that equaled or rivaled the role of the teacher. Hiring a technology consultant to manage the curriculum overrode the decision to hire two additional teachers who were desperately needed for math courses that went untaught. And when students struggled academically, the problem was framed as "product deficiency," and the proposed solution was for the school leaders to shop for another product rather than to incorporate obvious missing school structures (e.g., a teacher evaluation plan) to address the problem.

CRITICAL QUESTIONS

While blended learning has the potential to improve educational opportunities for students, the move to position it as a fix for educational inequities is fundamentally flawed both in conception and implementation.

What Is the Nature of the Curriculum, and What Is Worth Learning?

Blended education is often described on school websites as expanding pathways for learning for both teachers and students, because the design of the software enables teachers and students to "follow their interests." Students may switch from a math unit to a website on how math can be used to create apps or program a computer. However, the presence of the software itself does not widen students' access to knowledge. Curriculum that is commercially prepared may not be as interactive or as malleable as advertisements would suggest.

A key characteristic of any online curriculum is whether its architecture is open or closed. In the education technology space, open learning systems are intended to allow the user (the student) more control over the path of learning. This goes beyond stopping and starting as measured by minutes spent on the site. More open curriculum allows students to link to online activities and projects, videos, games that allow simulations, or other websites. In more closed systems, the user may have less control over the content. It may be difficult for the user to exit the curriculum due to restricted controls, or there may be more limited points of view presented in the curriculum (e.g., history or evolution).

The design of BA's program emphasized the flexibility of blended learning as it created opportunities for students to spend more time learning. But, giving low-income students greater access to technology does not address the resource inequities (limited access to computers and the Internet) that make this vision possible. Nor does the increased learning time argument address the often increased responsibilities for historically marginalized students (e.g., Justin's responsibility for himself and for his transient father). It doesn't solve the pragmatic and emotional problems of adolescents taking on more roles than their level of development can handle. If these students have extra responsibilities not shared by their middle- and upper-class peers *and* are expected to put in more time for school, what else is sacrificed?

Furthermore, BA's original design rightly criticizes deficit models where "broken students" are blamed for educational inequities but then points its finger at "programmatic and structural problems in school organizations" as causing dropouts. Moving from a student deficit theory to a school deficit theory still fails to identify the complex systems of inequities both within *and beyond* the school system that affect whether or not a particular student graduates high school. This neglect played out in BA's first year of operation, as critical analyses of race, gender, and class dropped out of the advisory curriculum and were replaced by increased Pyramid monitoring. It fell into the business-as-usual trap even though it was high tech, the curriculum was tested, and the teachers were highly qualified.

The Role of the Teacher in Driving Instruction

Blended education models are heralded as cost-saving measures because of reduced facility and labor costs given the curriculum's expected role as teacher. However, there can be hidden costs, and the ways in which public funds are distributed may not always be transparent. Hidden costs include the time spent by students and teachers learning the software in which the curriculum is housed. It can also include costs of technical support needed when the Internet goes down or the curriculum doesn't function in the way it is intended; this kind of technical support is rarely built into the lease of the curriculum. Vendor-controlled curriculum, such as that used in BA and schools across many states, may be expected to save teachers time (i.e., purchased curriculum allows more time for actual instruction), but, as the BA case illustrates, it has hidden costs for teachers in implementation.

BA's design heavily emphasizes student personalization, but it narrowly defines it as flexible pacing and varying course levels. In BA's first year of implementation, there was discussion early on about the project-based learning and advisory components of the school providing this sort of personalized, culturally responsive pedagogy. However, the school staff quickly deprioritized social-emotional components as the Pyramid-defined benchmarks created informal accountability systems for students and teachers. These programmatic decisions in the first year contributed to a perception that the digital curriculum was where the most "rigorous" content was delivered and to the assumption that teachers could rely on digital curriculum to differentiate content for students with different learning styles working at different levels and paces. This framing points to a transactional, commercial model of schooling, where seemingly neutral skills and concepts are drilled into students and other vital questions are left unaddressed.

The vendor controlled the curriculum and, in its failure to anticipate limitations of the curriculum, also controlled teachers. BA teachers, initially promised staggered work schedules, ended up working extended hours, often from 7:30 a.m. to 5:00 p.m. with expectations that they would stay later for afterschool activities and detention monitoring as well as maintain Saturday school hours. When it quickly became apparent to staff that students could not navigate the digital curriculum independently, most teachers shifted to a direct instruction mode of teaching; this shift led to a rigid bell schedule, and the teachers had no prep periods or breaks throughout the day other than a thirty-minute lunch period that they normally used for conferencing with or for student monitoring duty. Teachers felt the stress of too much work, which was compounded by their uncertain summer fate. The design had called for summer school, but teachers had no idea whether or not they would have a summer break beyond the two weeks of vacation allotted to them for the whole year.

As set out in the school's design, the on-site teachers (the state required one certified teacher for each room) were supposed to support "online master teachers" in the content areas, who were part of the digital curriculum package. This meant that the school budget could be stretched to hire more personnel, especially teaching assistants, to help the in-class teaching staff. However, in the school's implementation, this outsourcing and hiring of support staff did not happen as planned, and teachers had to pick up the slack of the content curriculum in addition to managing expectations to develop extensive advisory relationships and projects with smaller groups of students.

Who Owns the Data, and How Is Success Measured?

The working assumption on the part of the curriculum designers at Pyramid was that mastery would come as students worked through the course. In the words of the program designer, "If we assume mastery takes care of itself, teachers (and students) should focus most closely on on-scheduleness. If they stay on track with the calendar, they will successfully complete the course in a timely fashion. So, the red, yellow, green indicator becomes a proxy for that projection. It is a present time indicator. So, right now, if you are red, you are way behind expectations in your course and need to work harder to get your work done."

But in addition to there being problems with these indicators, this data offered little information on *what* students were or were not learning. It also provided little information on student behaviors linked to student performance. Though the digital curriculum was meant to be a helpful tool for teachers, too often the presence of technology and the lack of transparency around what students were each doing within Pyramid led to problems with student accountability and lack of progress—mastery. And because teachers often had a difficult time monitoring exactly what every student was and should have been doing in each class, several of them came up with their own ways of monitoring progress and mastery.

Vendors to blended education programs may advertise their services and products as comprehensive learning management systems with the capability to not only deliver content but also provide formative real-time feedback to students. And those systems may be sold to schools as "complete packages" that integrate operational and instructional sides of school operations—housing and aggregating enrollment data as well as data on student mastery and teacher performance. For staff and administrators who actually use the systems in classroom settings, software that helps on the front end (inputs) and the back end (outputs) is critical. But, equally critical are the processes that link the two. This goes beyond the presence or absence of software that can talk to each other. It concerns the human processes and interactions that help organize and facilitate updates of data, discussion of the data, and data's relevance and use in informing instruction. Comprehensive learning and course management systems ultimately depend on the will and capacity of effective administrators and staff to integrate software into live continuous dialogue on school improvement.

MISGUIDED PROMISES

If, as we argue, digital education is all about promises, then this case of a digital school raises the question of whether or not it might be a misguided promise for historically marginalized students like Justin, who struggle to find success in the complex interactions of teachers, students, administrators, and board members.

As Blended Academy progressed through its first year of operation, commercial decisions figured prominently in challenges like those faced by Justin, and the costs of these decisions were borne by school staff and by students. In this example, public schooling is the setting for blended education. Public funds are being used to support the school (whether federal, state, or local), and public policy and commercial interests are driving the changes. However, it is an ironic aspect of digital schooling that the "publicness" of the programs—the setting, the funding sources, and the interests—obscure the private and commercial influences driving these models and their expansion. The character of these investments, particularly in their emphasis on scalability over equity, may be a corruptive influence on the promise of digital education. The students at Blended Academy deserve the same access and quality programs as the primarily middle- and upper-class students enrolled in the Accelerated Blended Learning program.

CHAPTER 5

Policy Context and Commercial Decisions in Digital Tutoring

MAYA, A HIGH SCHOOL STUDENT in a large, midwestern school district, is sitting at the kitchen table with her mother. Together they are looking at the screen of a netbook. They have logged into the Project Achieve tutoring program software and are working through the first lesson. A prerecorded voice on the software program reads aloud: "Mark the word that is something that is sweet." Maya quickly chooses *candy* from the four options. "Mark the word that means 'to steer a car.'" Maya thinks it is *drive*, checks with her mom, and chooses the word. The program gives her four words and reads them aloud. It also asks her to read them after the program reads them, but it doesn't give much time; whenever she tries to read them aloud, she gets cut off by the program voice. Maya has stopped repeating them.

The program voice introduces another task: "Say these words after me. Mark the word that has the same vowel sound as sum." Maya guesses *group* and suggests it to her mom, but her mom isn't sure. She chooses *group*, which is wrong. This time her mom says the words aloud again. Maya isn't sure what *vowel* means; she's looking for a word with the *m* sound instead of the short *u* sound. Her mom repeats the instructions about vowel sounds but says she's not sure about the answers and that she's "really bad at this."

Maya attends a public school that is on what school staff call "the list." The school has not made state test score targets for at least three years and now, under the supplemental educational services provision of No Child Left Behind, is required to contract with outside vendors to provide free tutoring to low-income students, with tuition paid by the district out of federal Title I funds. Vendors can be almost any type of organization—public, private, for-profit, not-for-profit, secular, faith-based, local, or national. They can offer services in a number of formats, including online, software based, in person, at school sites, at home, or in community settings. Vendors go through an application process with the state and sign contracts with the districts. The policy mandates districts to contract with outside providers for these services. As with most other instructional contexts in K–12 education and beyond, digital education has become an important part of afterschool tutoring, which itself is a huge industry.

Market-based reform theories, with the assumption that market forces (choice and competition) promote accountability, are integral to the SES policy and much of NCLB. In the case of SES, this laissez fare approach limits state and district authority to monitor the quality of tutoring instruction. This high-commercial/low-accountability approach contributes to a situation where digital vendors are becoming some of the major providers of out-of-school time (OST) tutoring in large urban school districts. For example, in 2011–2012 a digital provider in one large district registered more than 17,000 students, capturing 22 percent of the market share. This is all happening within the context of constrained government oversight and with little evidence that digital instruction works better than face-to-face afterschool tutoring.

This chapter examines how digital formats can drive quality afterschool programming for students from low-income families by illustrating how the many decisions a vendor makes directly influence instruction.[1] And although many of these decisions seem technical (e.g., the type of hardware used to facilitate communication within the course) and are based on commercial incentives and not solely on educational goals and outcomes, they have a significant impact on the nature of digital instruction for the primarily low-income students they serve in the SES program. In the absence of policy allowing districts and states to regulate tutor qualifications, instructional formats, or even hourly rates, these decisions *become* the intervention.

In the same sense that policies made in Washington become interventions only when and as they are interpreted by those at the local level, there is a critical overlooked layer in digital education that fundamentally shapes the intervention students get—what they are taught, how they are taught, and how their mastery is assessed. These are not the kinds of high-level corporate decisions that get a lot of attention in much of the literature on privatization; they are intermediate and seemingly technical ones that have great impact on the instructional opportunities students actually receive.

Further, the case of digital tutoring reveals the problem of transparency in digital education. Parents can see what is happening because the tutoring may be happening in their home. At the same time, the online component may also make it more difficult for parents to fully grasp what is driving instruction, including who the child's tutor is and where the curriculum is coming from. And as for accountability, the counselor or assistant principal at Maya's school cannot simply do a walk-through of her tutoring session to see what she is getting, if there are technical problems, or even if Maya was in attendance.

DIGITAL TUTORING AS A CASE OF CONTRACTING FOR DIGITAL EDUCATION

Digital tutoring differs from digital courses and digital schools in that the intent is to supplement, not supplant, the traditional school instructional setting: students engage in digital tutoring to reinforce the skills and knowledge they learn during the school day; it takes place outside of the regular school hours and often at students' homes. Digital tutoring can include formats such as scheduled synchronous sessions via Internet-based software with a live tutor or asynchronous software loaded onto a netbook or handheld device that students work their way through on their own time.

Digital tutoring is at the intersection of two forms of instructional intervention: out-of-school time tutoring and digital education. Part of the challenge of assessing instructional quality in digital tutoring programs is the limited research base that specifically looks at where these two types of instruction overlap. The handful of studies examining the impact of different kinds of afterschool computer-based instruction on student outcomes show mixed results and seldom focus on the K–12 student population in the United States.[2] These findings on digital tutoring for school-age students should be interpreted with caution. We simply don't know enough on the use of technology in OST, as there is very little research specific to how digital formats can facilitate learning in OST contexts. However, we can look both to emerging research on quality digital education and the established research on the quality of OST experiences.[3]

In understanding digital tutoring as a type of digital education and the promise it may hold for students and schools, we have identified the following requirements for such a program:

- Teach and offer practice in the use of technology to build higher-order thinking skills such as analyzing, evaluating, creating, and applying. These skills involve, among other things, exercises in retrieving information on the Internet via blogs, searches, and websites.

- Differentiate among students' needs, connect to students' school days, organize in small grouping patterns, and keep instructional time consistent and sustained. Instructional strategies are varied, focused, sequenced, and explicit.

- Support positive relationships between and among students and parents, among tutors and students, and between the program and the community.

- Employ technology that is designed to be safe, operable, and accessible; can offer personalized, continuous feedback to students and teachers; and scaffolds activities in ways that account for different learning modalities.

These criteria frame how we examine OST instruction in digital settings and how we demonstrate the impact of vendors' decisions on the nature and quality of this instruction.

The SES provision of NCLB specifically targets students who are eligible for free and reduced-price lunch, which is the primary way districts and policy measure students' income status.[4] But while digital tutoring through SES has the potential to increase low-income students' access to supplemental instruction, it does not necessarily equate with increased opportunities *to learn*. These opportunities are enabled and constrained by vendors' decisions about the role of the tutor, the types of software used, and the hourly rates charged. For example, Project Achieve decided to not have a live tutor as part of its instructional design, leaving Maya without the support she needed to fully understand the material and requiring her mother to step in as her quasi-tutor.

In fact, there is a considerable and growing research base which suggests that SES (in both digital and nondigital formats) has little to no effect on student achievement. Specifically, looking across nearly a decade of research on SES, few studies find positive effects on student achievement, and where they do they are generally small, approximately a third of the effect size of similar interventions.[5] Research suggests that students have to participate in at least forty hours of SES a year to even start to see these minimal gains.[6] Importantly, studies suggest few students are receiving this minimum threshold of forty hours partly because of the hourly rates charged by tutoring vendors. Districts have a set per-pupil allotment to spend on SES tuition, so when some vendors charge twice as much as others, their students get half the number of tutoring hours. In addition, invoiced hours may not equate with actual hours of instruction received by students.[7] Again, SES offers a clear example of how policy structures (little regulatory power on the part of districts) and vendor decisions (hourly rates) directly impact students' opportunities to learn.

Findings of SES's minimal impact on student achievement, coupled with the mixed impacts of digital education in general, suggest that contracting for digital tutoring in a laissez-faire policy context can be an alarming waste of student instructional time and public funds.

Under the SES provision, the federal government mandates that districts with schools not meeting certain test score targets contract with outside vendors to provide tutoring. In other words, they must buy not make.[8] Specifically, the legislation states:

(3) AGREEMENT—In the case of the selection of an approved provider by a parent, the local educational agency shall enter into an agreement with such provider. Such agreement shall—

(A) require the local educational agency to develop, in consultation with parents (and the provider chosen by the parents), a statement of specific achievement goals for the student, how the student's progress will be measured, and a timetable for improving achievement that, in the case of a student with disabilities, is consistent with the student's individualized education program under section 614(d) of the Individuals with Disabilities Education Act;

(B) describe how the student's parents and the student's teacher or teachers will be regularly informed of the student's progress;

(C) provide for the termination of such agreement if the provider is unable to meet such goals and timetables.[9]

So whereas with the digital courses of Accelerated Blended Learning and the digital school, Blended Academy, policies may have facilitated education contracting for digital education, it did not require it. But through SES, underperforming districts have no choice but to contract for tutoring services, but they must contract with the providers approved by state agencies. And in most (if not all) cases, this includes vendors of digital tutoring services. Policy can facilitate or mandate educational contracting, but it can just as easily suppress it. In a clear illustration of the power of policy to create or curb markets, the amount of public funding available for contracting with third-party tutoring vendors under SES has dramatically decreased in those states granted waivers to certain NCLB provisions by the Department of Education. This means a considerable loss of revenue for tutoring companies that rely on SES contracts, prompting the industry to vigorously fight changes in SES legislation. In fact, Anne, a parent of a student enrolled in SES, reported that her child's tutoring provider called to tell her they were trying to get rid of free tutoring and then connected her directly to the city alderperson: "I mean, it was like a three-way [phone call]. They were on there . . . and I was on, yes, to make sure that I did talk to the alderman about keeping it, you know, telling him how important I thought it was and what my kids, how my kids progressed."

NCLB was passed in 2002, and the first districts with schools not meeting test score targets were required to offer SES beginning in 2004. In the case of SES, the state approves vendors' applications, the district signs contracts with vendors, parents sign an agreement with vendors to participate, and vendors of digital tutoring often have subcontracts, for example with hardware or software vendors.

One of the assumptions in educational contracting is that accountability partly comes through the contracting process itself; vendors and districts must make public the facts around a contract, the program it promises, and the standards to which it will be held.[10] In practice, however, we see a wide variety in the types and specificity of the terms in district contracts with SES vendors. These varied terms have an impact on the types of information parents, districts, and schools receive relative to the quality of the tutoring programs. For example, one district might include specific language about how much time a vendor has to enroll and begin services with a student before that student is enrolled with another vendor, and another district may not ask for any more specificity on program type than what is included in the state application.[11] Even if the information on program type and quality were specific and accurate, it is difficult to imagine parents navigating the complex processes of accessing these contracts to find out about programs. Also, districts are limited by SES policy in what they can require and therefore enforce in terms of instructional strategy and program structure. SES tutoring contracts illustrate not only the variance that can result when policies take a laissez-faire approach but its implications for the quantity and quality of information available to stakeholders, such as districts and parents.

WHAT DRIVES DIGITAL TUTORING?

Maya and her parents had a range of options when it came to choosing a tutoring provider. They most likely received a booklet in the mail from the school district in which each page described a different provider. Some were digital and some not; some had school-based programs and others took place at home. What about these descriptions of digital tutoring compelled Maya to enroll with Project Achieve? What does it mean when a program says it is "software-based" or when another vendor, Virtual Tutors, says it uses "live instructors"? What is the universe of possible formats in a digital tutoring program? To what extent does the description that vendors of digital tutoring provide match what happens in practice? These can be rather straight-forward questions in a traditional tutoring setting, where a tutor or teacher instructs by implementing a curriculum. But our fieldwork shows just how very different this can be in the context of digital learning, primarily because of the software that implements curriculum, either in conjunction with a live tutor or totally absent one.

Instructional Format and the Role of the Tutor

The first variable in understanding the nature of digital tutoring is the instructional format, which includes the role of the tutor. Trying to gauge this based simply on program descriptions, such as the ones Maya and her parents may have read, can be difficult because of a lack of detailed and sometimes contradictory information provided by vendors in state applications, district contracts, and marketing materials. SES is a classic case of how digital education can offer much data but too little useful information.

We have identified two primary formats of digital tutoring:

- Digital instruction
  - *Synchronous.* Live tutor using either a course management system (CMS) or structured curriculum-based software that the student and tutor work through together
  - *Asynchronous.* Student works mostly independently through either online or static curriculum-based software

- Tutoring session
  - *All digital*
  - *Blended digital and in-person*

We also looked at the role of the tutor. Again, digital education confounds the traditional idea of teacher or tutor. Digital tutors can play a broad spectrum of roles. We define *tutor* as the provider staff most directly responsible for the instruction of an individual student and categorize the various roles of the tutor as:[12]

- *No tutor.* In some digital tutoring platforms students have no interaction with a human during the tutoring session. Instead, students interact with instructional software and may have the option of calling a helpline if they get stuck on a problem. Students also might interact with a vendor staff member on occasion to upload progress reports or deal with technical needs.
- *Technician.* Some tutoring platforms use personnel only for technical assistance, which could include a technical helpline or delivering/retrieving hardware from students' homes. We also observed sessions where students brought netbooks into a central location to have provider personnel upload their work progress through preloaded software.
- *Monitor/Guide.* Beyond a technician but not quite a full, interactive instructor, the monitor responds to students if they need help on a specific question related to academic content, calls families to discuss progress, encourages students, and answers questions via e-mail.
- *Instructor.* A tutor is an instructor if the tutor interacts with a student throughout the session and if the curriculum could not progress without the tutor. The tutor is an integral part of the instructional platform and curriculum delivery.

In practice, tutors often occupy multiple categories, sometimes simultaneously.

Curriculum and Assessment

It is important to remember that digital education makes traditional distinctions between curriculum and instruction more complex. For example, when there is no live tutor, in some formats the software and curriculum become the tutor, as they are what drive instruction.

Although the general content focus is always either language arts or math (per SES regulatory guidance), the specific formats used by vendors run along a spectrum. Many vendors focus on building and practicing foundational skills (e.g., verb tenses or adding fractions). The curricular formats across vendors range from highly structured and completely dependent on the software to "homegrown" curriculum that is more fluid and dependent on the discretion of a live tutor. The curriculum used by digital vendors comes from a variety of sources. A number of vendors have developed their own proprietary curriculum that is only used by their tutors. Others have either purchased an entire packaged curriculum embedded in a software system and pay to maintain its license or use a combination of purchased and homegrown content.

By law, all SES tutoring vendors, digital or nondigital, must provide each student with pre- and post-test scores as part of their curricula. Of those providers we studied, vendors develop digital assessments in-house, purchase them from another company, or use district assessments as pre- and post-tests. For those vendors administering their own pre- and post-tests, assessments are in a digital format (except in the case of one vendor that conducts verbal assessments of kindergarten and first grade students, who might have problems navigating the digital platform). A number of the vendors we sampled also use formative assessments throughout the program to measure progress and potentially revise the scope and sequence of a student's learning plan. These formative assessments are often short sets of problems designed to gauge whether students understood a concept; software stops a student from moving forward unless they respond correctly or a live tutor approves their progress and moves them on to the next activity.

In all cases we studied, the vendor of digital tutoring controlled decisions around assessment data with few boundaries placed by the SES policy provision itself and therefore little oversight by districts or states. With the exception of the one district where vendors used the standard district assessment, vendors determine, create or purchase, administer, and report the results of the pre- and post-assessments to establish whether or not their program is impacting student learning.

This results in a patchwork of assessments with little to no validity in determining whether this multimillion dollar intervention is working.

Software and Hardware Options

Software is central to digital tutoring platforms. We observed three different types of software used to facilitate instructional interactions among students, tutors, and curriculum:

- *Synchronous instructional software* facilitates live instructional interaction between students and tutors through chat functions, audio capabilities, and/or a whiteboard function. In the case of the vendors in our study, the software houses the curricular content itself. This type of software typically could generate progress reports.
- *Synchronous course management system software* facilitates live interaction between students and tutors, in one case through a whiteboard platform combined with an Internet-based voice call service (e.g., Skype). This type of software simply offers a platform that facilitates digital interaction between student and tutor, but the tutor generates or delivers homegrown curricular content.
- *Asynchronous instructional software* provides curricular content but does not support live interaction between students and tutors. It houses assessments, generates progress reports, and, in many cases, uses artificial intelligence to adapt the course based on student responses.

In some cases, software is developed by the provider itself or with a subcontracted developer. In other cases, providers purchase or lease preexisting software from other firms.[13]

The need for some level of hardware to facilitate instruction is endemic to the digital tutoring context and to all forms of digital education. The type of hardware used by vendors in our study depends on the particular instructional platform but includes mp3 players (e.g., iPods), tablets, netbooks, laptops, and desktops. Some vendors send desktops or laptops (with headphones) to students' homes for them to access the instructional program online. Another vendor gives students iPods loaded with instructional software. The sources of hardware differ by provider. Some have purchasing agreements with particular computer companies for new equipment, while others purchase refurbished handhelds or laptops.

Digital instruction requires other hardware needs as well, such as an Internet connection. All but one of the vendors in our qualitative sample requires an Internet connection in order for instruction to take place, which is provided through the school where the tutoring session takes place or in a student's home. All vendors in our sample either provide or pay for an Internet connection either in students' homes or via devices such as aircards that use cellular networks to access the Internet.

And so it becomes clear how otherwise seemingly technical decisions about hardware impact students' opportunities to learn. Imagine using the small screen of a handheld device, such as an iPod, to read passages and respond to comprehension questions during an hour-long tutoring session. And although some students might prefer the flexibility of not needing an Internet connection to complete their work, consider the impact of the decision whether or not to incorporate the Internet as part of the tutoring program, and the subsequent decision whether or not to provide it, on the nature of instruction. In the absence of regulation, these key decisions around access are left up to vendors.

MAPPING THE DECISIONS THAT MATTER IN DIGITAL TUTORING

As the previous two cases suggest, the decisions digital education vendors make in the absence of government oversight matter to the nature of digital instruction. But the case of digital tutoring even more strongly demonstrates the impact of these decisions, partly because we are able compare different vendors and formats within the same context and see how they play out in practice. Using three "portraits" based on observations and interviews, we address two critical questions: What types of decisions do digital tutoring vendors make when it comes to format and the role of the tutor, curriculum, assessments, hardware, and software? And how do these decisions impact opportunities to learn for the low-income students enrolled in their programs?

1. Computer Tutors: When the Tutor Drives Instruction

Computer Tutors is a for-profit vendor of synchronous digital tutoring serving students in districts across the country. It relies on a CMS to house a curriculum primarily driven and delivered by a live tutor. Computer Tutors uses a CMS that essentially is a digital whiteboard, accessible to students via the Internet and where they interact with a live tutor through Internet-based phone calls using audio headsets. Tutors ask questions and give instructions through both the audio and whiteboard functions, while students write and respond on this digital whiteboard. In the excerpt below, a tutor describes the technology and how it structures interactions among the student, tutor, and curriculum:

> This thing has a speaker and also has a microphone, so every, *every* student is sitting in front of their computer. Here's the speakers where they can listen to the tutor, and here's the microphone . . . So it's like, very much like a live interaction, and they also see— we have something called like an online whiteboard. So they see the exact same stuff that the tutor is looking at, so there's no time lag, it's instant, it's real time, it's based on Flash technology. It's fairly—it's actually totally real time, so if they write something on that whiteboard, using either their mouse or electronic notepad or something, the tutor sees it right away.

If you follow this technology into homes and sit next to students as they work on it, what will you see? The following is an excerpt from an observation of a tutoring session in the home of a student enrolled in Computer Tutors; it describes in detail how these intended interactions play out in real time. The student, Vicki, signed onto the Internet via a computer provided by Computer Tutors and interacted with the tutor using an audio headset also provided by the vendor.

The tutor says, "Okay, now this one." Vicki rewrites the problem from the worksheet freehand on the online whiteboard, multiplying the denominators in her head and also the numerators. She finishes. The tutor quietly says, "Very good. Now the next one." It is a story problem. The tutor does not have Vicki read it out loud or ask her what the problem is looking for. As she writes out the problem, the tutor corrects her to add instead of subtract. Vicki starts to change both denominators, but she only needed to change one, the tutor explains. The tutor finishes the problem, "So it's 3/8, isn't it," and Vicki says, "Yeah." The tutor asks if she is okay; she says "yeah" and goes on to the next problem.

Vicki interacts directly with and manipulates the content of the curriculum by writing, evaluating, and then changing her work on the digital whiteboard, all the time interacting with the tutor who is providing feedback through this same platform. The interaction is in real time and requires participation from both Vicki and her tutor.

Computer Tutors decided to structure its digital tutoring so that the tutor drives the delivery, pace, and, at times, the content of the curriculum. Yet this decision has trade-offs, as the open-ended nature of the platform turns heavily on tutor capacity. This is an important consideration, when the type of constructivist instruction demands a high level of teacher expertise and time. This particular choice of format, facilitated by the choice of CMS, not only allows more flexibility on the part of the tutor to incorporate differentiated instruction but also offers multiple ways to interact with students. The technology itself (CMS software using a whiteboard and audio connection) allows for continuous feedback from the tutor as well as differentiation and adaptation to student needs. A tutor offers an example: "With the younger lot, you know, the 3rd, 4th, and the 5th grade especially, I've found that we have to make the session more interactive, more such drawings, and more such, you know, we cannot upload videos and things like that, it's not right, because the child gets distracted." He is able to adapt how he delivers content based on the age (and distractibility) of the student. Computer Tutors also ensures that a tutor only works with one student at a time and that students stay paired with the same tutor throughout all tutoring sessions, which is not the case with all digital tutoring providers. Its decision to use a CMS with live tutors means the curriculum can be more easily differentiated and students can have a chance to develop and sustain supportive interactions with tutors.

But there are other aspects of Computer Tutors that suggest more limited student access to transformative digital instruction. Namely, the content of the curriculum itself is based on skill-building tasks that essentially equate to worksheets. Whereas students might learn new skills in using a digital whiteboard and remote audio connections, this model does not use the technology itself to develop higher-order skills (analyzing, evaluating, creating, and applying information from the Internet). The vendor has set up a structure where tutors have the flexibility to create more innovative curriculum but does not set expectations or provide the necessary resources to support tutors in doing this.

2. Virtual Tutors: Live Tutors with Scripted Curriculum

Virtual Tutors is a national for-profit company that uses an online platform with curriculum-based software. Students interact with both a live tutor and instructional software, and the instruction is jointly driven by a live tutor and the software. In these mixed contexts, students see and move through an online curriculum that has a series of skill explanations, then practice problems, and finally a brief formative assessment. Tutors are actively involved in the process, explaining directions and correcting work. Tutors may direct some of the scope and sequence in that they can determine if students skip certain questions or get additional practice, but unlike Computer Tutors, instructors with Virtual Tutors do not generate any of the curriculum content. Curriculum developers at the corporate level of Virtual Tutors generate standardized curriculum used with all students. Students at various ages and ability levels are assigned different segments of the curriculum and move through it at different speeds.

An observation of a Virtual Tutors session with two students, Paul and Kaila, illustrate how the curriculum-based software dictates more of the interaction between tutor and student than a basic CMS might in settings like Computer Tutors: "The activity asked Kaila to use positive and negative integers in word problems related to the height and flow of rivers. The tutor did the first problem together with Kaila, told her to work on her own, and then moved over to Paul who was in the middle of another exercise using word problems." The curriculum software developed by Virtual Tutors allows tutors to work with up to three students at the same time during a single one-hour tutoring session. They move among separate "classrooms," checking in on student progress and providing guidance as needed:

> The tutor checked over them, said Paul was doing really well on his own and that she appreciated it. She talked through one question with him and then switched back to Kaila. While back with Kaila she talked through a couple of the integer problems. She would ask set-up questions building up to the answer. She would ask her to highlight or circle the parts of the word problem she needs to work with to answer the question. The tutor gave lots of praise to Kaila, verbally and with online "tokens," which can be used to redeem small, educational prizes. The answer key is on the right side of the tutor's screen and the tutor will click "accurate" or "not accurate" for each problem depending on how the student answers. The student cannot move on to another activity without 80 percent "mastery."

Virtual Tutors' decisions around the type of software and platform limit students to only interacting with the tutor, not with other students. Therefore, students primarily work independently through the sequenced curriculum but depend on the tutor to move them on to subsequent sections or to explain and demonstrate challenging concepts. A tutor describes how this works in practice:

> Some of the lessons are guided practices where the teacher walks them through a new skill. Some of them are independent practices or problem solving, where they apply what they've been learning and they basically work on their own, and the teacher pops in between the kids. There is what we call a "view" tool, where a teacher can actually be talking to one student and looking at another student's

work and typing little comments to them. So it's easy to stay in contact with all of your students at once.

Virtual Tutors offers a different illustration of the impact of the decisions digital tutoring vendors make about format and curriculum. For example, the software in this model structures a much more sequenced and explicit curriculum than the CMS that Computer Tutors uses. Yet, the trade-off here is that tutors have limited discretion over the content or structure of the curriculum. Their interaction with the curriculum is primarily to guide students through it—introducing, reviewing, and evaluating the skills in the lesson. When they do have flexibility, it is in the form of adapting the pace or number of problems assigned, with some space for inserting extra problems of their own. This provider only hires certified teachers and requires a certain amount of classroom teaching experience, yet the tutors are limited in their ability to use this increased capacity. One tutor lamented:

> There isn't a whole lot of prep work other than making sure your technology is working properly, your hardware, your Internet service, because of the way the program is designed, it's very prescriptive, so when the pre-assessment is done, children are placed, a very individualized learning program is put into the system for them, and I don't mean to sound negative but it's sort of like you could be a monkey. And [to] administer this, I think it's good to have background teaching techniques—things like higher level questioning, basic classroom management strategies, basic instruction strategies, but it's so specific in what you need to do, it . . . You don't have to be a high-functioning teacher to do that.

Tutors do, however, have a number of digital avenues through which to communicate with students (including audio, whiteboard, and chat functions), and the software allows for constant feedback. We observed positive rapport between students and tutors in a number of sessions, but, unlike Computer Tutors, students are seldom matched with the same tutor from session to session. While the tutors and other instructional staff interact through software to exchange information about students, the students do not have a consistent presence, and therefore this model does not facilitate the development of meaningful student-teacher relationship building within the instructional setting. This limitation was noted by a number of tutors: "One of the things I don't like about the program is that it's different kids all the time. And so I feel like, at least it's been my experience, most of teaching especially—it really is about building relationships. And you don't get to do that on here." The Virtual Tutors model allows for plenty of interaction between tutor and student during a single session, but the important trade-off here is that this interaction is not sustained. It cannot build over time. And we know that the ability to create relationships with students is critical to effective teaching.

Virtual Tutor's technology and software is impressive. Students access well-organized, sequenced curriculum that is based on pre-assessments. Yet this model begs the question of whether the technology is driving innovative and transformative digital instruction or just delivering traditional instruction in a different package. Students might learn how to use the hardware (laptops and headsets) and navigate a learning platform, but, as with Computer Tutors, students are not asked to use the technology toward higher-order thinking skills.[14]

3. Project Achieve, eTutors, and Progress Learning: When Software Drives Instruction

With Project Achieve, eTutors, and Progress Learning, three asynchronous vendors, while there may be tutoring staff available via phone or chat for questions, instruction, as well as curriculum, is fully driven by the software. Students take an assessment with the vendor, and, based on the results, the software creates a curriculum program for the student. The students either log in on their own time and work through the software or log in during group sessions at common sites, like a school.

Maya is enrolled in Project Achieve, an asynchronous digital tutoring program that uses software to structure how Maya interacts with the curriculum. The curriculum becomes even more central when there is no consistent, live tutor working between students and the curriculum. In this case, Maya's mother acted as a quasi-tutor to facilitate the instruction. Project Achieve staff act more as monitors or guides, calling students once a week to discuss their progress, offer encouragement, and answer questions. A Project Achieve tutor sees the limitations in structuring student interactions this way:

> And it's hard, because we're here but we're not. Because everything is online and it's up to them to know. I mean, they can always ask me, but at the same point I don't exactly know where they're at in the program, and then also, I wish we had some kind of other deal where we could at least see them online, and see them working, or however that would work out. Because, I mean, it works, but it just seems like if they're really struggling that they should be doing a different type of tutoring, you know, more one-on-one.

This same tutor also expressed frustration over how they interact with students via e-mail about instructional and administrative questions:

> So a lot of times I get a lot of e-mails from students and they'll ask me questions like how many hours do I have or how do I work this problem out. And I would send them some examples through the e-mail. You know, give them some subtraction problems if that's what they were having trouble with, and I tell them to fill it out and send it back to me. And I would tell them what they got right and what they got wrong. And usually when I try to talk to them on the phone if they're having a problem in a certain area, I'll go through the problems, you know, make up my own and go through with them to make sure they understand. But I mean it sometimes is—it is hard to explain more when you're on the phone, when you can't see somebody and write it out.

Although Project Achieve has built in a way for students to ask questions, the choice of hardware (i.e., telephone) seriously limits the ability of tutors to respond in any sort of substantive way. Also, opportunities to develop positive and productive relationships are essentially impossible in this setting. Similarly, Progress Learning is another vendor that offers asynchronous tutoring using curriculum-based software, where interactions between students and live staff typically are brief and only happen once a week. And when tutors and students do interact, it might just be around logistical or technical issues as opposed to instructional issues. This is a central limitation to an asynchronous digital tutoring format.

Another major question about this format is whether or not it truly can adapt to student needs. All of the asynchronous curriculum-based software programs in our sample relied on software that is designed to react and adapt to student responses. For example, an administrator from eTutors explained how its curriculum software achieves this:

> [The programs] have an artificial intelligence that learns the students' different areas of weaknesses—that remediates those at a student-specific level . . . It really is a learning tool, but what it does is you answer the question, kind of similar to the GMAT. It asks you hard or easier questions based on your responses and then we have a component in there that notices if you keep missing questions with the word "right" in it, like "right angle" or "right triangle," then it realizes that that's where your area of difficulty is and continues asking questions to remediate that until it sees that you've been successful.

Some might argue that asynchronous digital tutoring curriculum can offer opportunities to learn for students in that they are based on structured, explicit, and sequenced curriculum that "adapts" to student learning. But the extent to which this curriculum can align to students' day school instruction and truly adjust to their instructional (let alone social and emotional) needs is questionable, beyond simply changing the pace or particular single-item response questions the student is expected to answer. And unlike the asynchronous digital courses described in chapter 3, the asynchronous, software-driven curriculum, as illustrated by these three providers, does not encourage students to use the technology in the actual content of their learning. In other words, students are not asked to make the technology central to employing higher-order thinking skills.

CRITICAL QUESTIONS

In the case of digital tutoring, vendors are confronted with a host of trade-offs when making very different kinds of decisions about what will drive curriculum and instruction. These decisions around curriculum, instruction, the tutor, assessments, software, and hardware matter to the quality of digital tutoring, particularly in targeting low-income students. These are important decisions for districts to consider when signing contracts with vendors. The variation across vendors in approaches to curriculum, instruction, and assessment and data systems makes for a complex landscape of options for districts, and figure I.1 is helpful in prompting critical dialogue and determining the types of digital tutoring programs that best fit their students' needs and district goals. For example, the farther down one gets along the Y axis of "instruction" toward "software driven" (e.g., Project Achieve, eTutors, Progress Learning) the less likely that sustained and supporting relationships can occur for students within the digital setting, relationships that may be key to keeping students engaged with the actual intervention.

What Drives Digital Curriculum and Instruction, and What Is the Role of the Tutor?

Digital tutoring offers a clear example of the complexity in determining what drives digital instruction. The three portraits detail digital formats that blur distinctions between curriculum and instruction and between the role of software and tutors. For example, instead of using live tutors, the vendors in Portrait 3 decided to rely on asynchronous, curriculum-based software. This leads to limitations in the ability of instructors to develop supportive relationships with students, an element that is critical to effective learning in OST settings. In contrast, the other two portraits describe digital tutoring that uses live tutors, which allows for increased communication.

Yet, simply making the decision to have a live tutor using a CMS does not ensure quality communication between tutor and student or increased opportunities to learn. Tutors must be well-trained and given time to develop a curriculum that requires higher-order thinking and meaningful interaction with students. By way of comparison, the online portion of Accelerated Blended Learning courses would inhabit a similar space on figure I.1 as Computer Tutors, but ABL exhibits a much more innovative and transformative digital instructional experience than Computer Tutors. There certainly are instances of digital tutoring offering quality instruction of the skill-drilling nature. But while the curriculum might be at an appropriate level of rigor, be aligned to standards, and be delivered by a live tutor, it still lacks the innovation promised by advocates of digital education, whereas ABL leveraged flexible CMS and active teacher roles to demand higher-order tasks of students and truly *use* the technology toward greater learning.

What Drives Assessment, and Who Has Access to What Data?

Assessment and the data it generates are just as important a consideration in digital tutoring as curriculum and instruction, and just as complex. The distinctions among curriculum, instruction, and assessment are often unclear, especially for programs where the software drives the assessment, which drives aspects of the curriculum, which drives instruction. For example, an administrator from Progress Learning explains the limitations of a model where software drives curriculum, instruction, and assessment:

> Obviously technology is a good piece to it, but we can't simply rely all on technology. Because let's say the student was very hasty on the initial test, and they just basically marked Cs all across the board, right? Which is entirely possible. And it's happened to us before (laughs). My curriculum will be designed based on the answers that he/she has given to us. Now the student might receive a laptop that's too hard for them, or perhaps too easy for them.

The quality and relevance of the curriculum *and* instruction in this model completely depend on how accurate the assessment is.

One of the promises of digital education is to use technology to harness "big data" and create more refined assessments that can impact instruction. Yet, there is evidence that large digital vendors have not mastered even the basics of data use toward learning. For example, Tanya, a mother of a high school student struggling in geometry, signed her son up for an asynchronous online tutoring program:

> It turned out that it was actually no help. It actually took him away, time away, from his regular studies, because this was a company that called every day, every evening, to see if he was online. Every day. And it was so annoying, because he would come home. He'd have to do his regular work. And they would call and [say], "Are you the parent?" And, "We want to make sure you signed on." Sometimes he had already signed on and finished the assignment, and it's like there were no checks and balances . . . And I'm like, "What do you need to know? He's signed in. Can't you check? Can't you monitor from your end?" But like clockwork, he would call every day.

Digital vendors have an incentive to make sure students are signed on and complete the daily work; this is how they invoice districts and ultimately get paid. In this case, the vendor did not provide accurate attendance data to the person charged with calling to check on student progress. And these calls created constant frustration for Tanya and her family, who felt that this distraction actually negatively impacted her son's ability to finish homework from his day school.

Apart from assessment and progress data, the types of information and data provided by vendors to the states and districts, let alone the parents of eligible students, are mixed. It is difficult to piece together from district budgets and provider reports what money is being spent where. Furthermore, the information available from different levels of government can be inconsistent, as program descriptions from state vendor applications might differ from the information asked for and detailed in district contracts. The information parents receive about vendor programs can be watered down and misleading. For example, a vendor might say it provides services for students with disabilities but does not actually hire tutors with special education training. Vendor program descriptions provide minimal information for parents on how they use technology as part of instruction. These factors, along with the challenges in "entering" a digital tutoring site, add to the troubling lack of transparency in digital tutoring.

Ultimately, the stories of Maya and all the other students promised greater opportunities to learn through choosing digital tutoring illustrate how vendor decisions matter a great deal to the quality of instruction for students from low-income families. And other more technical decisions, not so easily defined as instructional decisions, can matter just as much. The hourly rates charged by providers are a great example of how technical decisions translate directly to instructional impacts. As a result of the geometric relationship between the per-pupil allotment that can be spent on SES tuition and the unregulated hourly rates charged by providers, most of the students in our study received well below the forty hours of tutoring that is the minimum threshold for realizing any gain on academic achievement. Decisions around hourly rates lead directly and literally to a decreased opportunity to learn in the form of fewer hours of instruction. There are implications for data use in this example as well, since the system of charging by the hour typically means vendors control the collection and reporting of attendance (and therefore invoice) information to districts. Understaffed district offices neither have the time nor resources to monitor every student's attendance and whether it is accurately reported on vendors' invoices.[15]

Why do these decisions matter? They either structure learning for students in the skill drills of the typical worksheet or begin to fulfill the promise of digital education to facilitate innovative and transformative learning. These decisions either perpetuate the most uninspired instruction many low-income students receive or truly disrupt it. They structure the pricing of their services either to maximize their profit margin or to maximize the learning potential for students.

Each of these decisions involves give and take, but are they commercial trade-offs or educational ones? In the absence of policy directives on important areas such as the availability of live, experienced tutors or the alignment of curriculum to students' day school instruction, the decisions are solely in the hands of vendors. So what are the downstream users of digital education to do? Are these the kinds of decisions where there could be more standard setting or guidance that provides incentives for vendors to translate technological decisions into instructional ones? Is there any way for districts, teachers, students, and their parents to begin to structure a dialogue around digital education that leads to truly transformative learning for low-income students?

The answer is yes.

PART THREE

Shifting the Current

CHAPTER 6

Changing the Dialogue

Tools for Building Transparency and Accountability in Digital Education for Students in Low-Income Settings

DURING A PROFESSIONAL development meeting toward the end of Blended Academy's first year, Dr. M. continues his presentation on teacher evaluations: "Okay, let's go to presenting instructional content. What will be expected of you? This isn't yet aligned to a blended learning model, so we may need to adjust it." As he moves to his next slide, teachers' hands go up and questions start emerging. "So in presenting content, what are we looking for?" asks one teacher, explaining, "We're supposed to be an individualized school, but what does that look like in an evaluation rubric?" Another teacher interjects, "Are we expecting teachers to rely on Pyramid for the presentation of content? Or are we saying that the teachers are responsible?" Dr. M. thinks for a moment before responding, "We need to curate Pyramid. Sometimes Pyramid isn't going to be sufficient." Yet another teacher responds, "If you're just looking at Pyramid, you're evaluating Pyramid, not the teacher."

Dr. M. acknowledges that negotiating teacher evaluation around the school's Pyramid digital curriculum will be the hard part of the staff's dialogue around teacher evaluations. He notes that these particular questions seem to be focused around the planning end of teacher performance. The first teacher shares, "But a lot of that individual stuff is not planned." Dr. M. replies, "Well, that may fall under knowledge of a student." "That's differentiation," the teacher quips. As the conversation continues, Dr. M. faces the teachers' concerns head-on and makes note of questions that need to be addressed in order for BA to have an effective system for teacher evaluation. This interchange illustrates a teacher-initiated dialogue as the staff tries to find ways to better connect the commercial curriculum with nature of their work, the complexity of teaching, and the potential of digital education.

In the preceding chapters we have explored three distinct settings of digital education: digital courses, digital schools, and digital tutoring. Our purpose has been to look within the instructional setting—at the kinds of things that shape it in very important ways—to see what students get from public schools, specifically where digital education has replaced traditional brick-and-mortar classrooms. Michael Horn, among others, has referred to the dynamic by which new players enter the education market and sell new, digital modes of instruction, curriculum, and assessment as "disruptive innovation." The theory is that the competitive dynamic of these firms, with the best rising to the top, can significantly alter the distribution of quality instruction in U.S. public schools by beaming high-quality teachers into low-income communities to "teach," thereby increasing the supply of teachers in communities where shortages are acute.

Indeed, in all three cases we see digital education disrupting classroom routines and practices: the role of the teacher and implications for instruction, access to and the content of curriculum, what students are expected to know, the role of data and implications for assessment, and what kind and quality of data is used to assess student and teacher performance. But in each case there are few indications that digital education has moved the needle in any significant way toward increasing opportunities to learn for low-income students.

Transformative education through digital education is a possibility, but in the two settings we studied where the target group was low-income students, digital schools and digital tutoring, there appears to be little policy incentive or commercial pressure to make digital education work for low-income populations. And in the third case, digital courses, high-functioning blended instruction was not equally serving low-income students in the target population. We found that within the context of high-functioning digital education for a particular population of students provided by a nonprofit contractor, districts and vendors face challenges in connecting this instruction with low-income students.

We contend that through dialogue we can make changes in these settings so that transformative digital education becomes a part of a systematic effort to increase access and quality of learning opportunities for low-income students. There are very promising examples of such a dialogue in two of these cases, while in the other there are clear reasons why the dialogue has not progressed as far, though there are some signs of forward movement. In this chapter we look at how real people at the ground level of the implementation of digital education—or those downstream—are dealing with the challenges we highlighted in our case studies. We detail how vendors and end users can create productive dialogue on the critical questions around what drives curriculum, instruction, assessment, and the use of data. Ultimately, these conversations are toward the goal of holding digital education accountable to standards of high quality and access for all students.

The local contexts and types of digital education described in chapters 3–5 differ in important ways. Despite these differences, key stakeholders in each setting used similar strategies to build greater transparency around the nature and quality of curriculum, instruction, and assessment in digital education, pushing for greater access to quality instruction for low-income students. These common strategies for engaging in productive dialogue across settings included:

- Use of evidence
- Movement of parents, teachers, and students from consumers to producers of data on digital education
- Creation of accountability tools
- Leverage of support by agents with initial resources (time and money) to build evidence and broker demands.

FIGURE 6.1   Strategies to build dialogue around quality and access in digital education

Agent	Producing data	Creating tools	Engaging with research	Outcome
District Staff	Monitoring sessions; stakeholder surveys	Classroom observation tools	Review research base; university research partnerships	Minimal *standards* for instructor qualifications, instructor-to-student ratio, and hours of instruction offered
School Staff	Documenting teacher and student voices	Authentic assignments; archiving teacher e-mail	University research partnerships	Inclusion of *user voice* in structured discussions and resulting questions about the quality and accessibility of leased digital curriculum
Vendors	Listening sessions; program data on participation and satisfaction	Structured feedback loops via reports of course data to districts	Review research base; university research partnerships	Build *vendor capacity* through better data collection for student demographics, action plan for course structure, and professional development for instructors

In each of the settings, the dialogue, combined with practical strategies to move from dialogue to action, altered the dynamics, laying the groundwork for a more public lens through which teachers, parents, and students could view vendor and government actions (see figure 6.1).

RIVER CITY SCHOOL DISTRICT: LEVERAGING EVIDENCE, STAKEHOLDERS, AND TOOLS

River City Public Schools (RCPS) is one of the many school districts across the country that was required to provide eligible students in schools failing to meet adequate yearly progress with free afterschool tutoring through the supplemental educational services provision. Per

NCLB requirements, RCPS contracted with state-approved tutoring providers between 2005 and 2012, paying providers for the hours students attended tutoring sessions. Under the regulatory guidance, districts had little ability to regulate the format or conditions of SES tutoring. For example, RCPS could not limit the hourly rates charged by providers, which ranged from $55 to $102 in 2010–2011, with an average of $80 per hour. Since the total amount the district could spend for one student's tutoring depended on a per-pupil allotment determined by the state, hourly rates were directly associated with total possible hours, averaging fewer than twenty-five hours each year. In addition, RCPS could not put minimum requirements on tutor qualifications, the curriculum used, nor the instructional format.[1] Districts like RCPS were forced by federal law to enter into contracts with vendors even though they had minimal control over the terms of these agreements and little ability to enforce them.

In the early years following NCLB implementation, RCPS became a magnet for preexisting and new vendors of afterschool tutoring because of its high concentration of "failing" schools. Vendors of afterschool tutoring programs sent sales teams to the city's low-income neighborhoods to recruit students for the program. Vendors who offered incentives to parents and families for enrolling in the program grew their market share, creating a contentious atmosphere where providers competed aggressively for students and hurled accusations of malfeasance. The dynamics of vendor influence rose along with digital education. Digital vendors were able to gain market share by offering families incentives, such as a free computer. The idea of tutoring at home during flexible hours often appealed to families concerned about safe transportation home from school or conflicts with other responsibilities, such as afterschool jobs and caring for younger siblings.

Seeking Greater Transparency and Accountability

As field researchers in the setting, we struggled to understand the instructional approaches and impacts of some of the large digital providers. Because digital tutoring was not, for the most part, happening in school settings, we could not "sit in on" a session like we did with nondigital providers. Therefore, it was hard for both us and the district to even get a sense of the critical areas of curriculum, instruction, tutor interaction, and assessment, let alone understand the logistics of how students actually accessed the instructional platform. In addition, the tutors in this instance were not local—people we could observe, greet, and have conversations with after a tutoring session as students were leaving. They were, by and large, faceless teachers geographically dispersed across the country and identified to students on a first name basis.

Initially, we gained access to the instructional settings of one large national provider by watching sessions on a company computer at a regional office using the "voyeur" function. But the company closed its River City office, deciding it was more cost-efficient to have the larger, regional office run the River City programs. From 2009 to 2012, the only way we were able to access a live instructional setting was by going through the district, asking them to request a "monitoring session" (which providers typically granted only one per year per district), which involved us sitting in on a live session remotely from our office computer via a webinar platform. There typically were three or four corporate staff on the call during these observations, including the director of academic instruction, which afforded us the opportunity to talk with the vendor about these critical areas of curriculum, instruction, and assessment while watching how tutors interacted with students. While these sessions gave us a sense of what was happening, much remained opaque.[2] And the district, too, was also was growing increasingly interested in transparency, in the fairness and openness of all providers' activities in the district.

In an effort to increase accountability for all tutoring providers, the director of Extended Learning Opportunities (ELO) for RCPS had her staff check through provider invoices to compare them to the actual hours students attended sessions. The district administrators grew increasingly frustrated that the state did not take a more active or aggressive role in regulating providers or putting tighter rules in place, although rules had been added that curtailed the types of incentives providers could use. In addition, RCPS moved to require that all vendors use districtwide assessments, administered in the fall, winter, and spring, as their pre- and post-tests instead of the each vendor using its own assessment system. The district also formed a steering committee to look at ways of improving SES, which came partly out of the initiative of a community organization interested in improving access to and the quality of free afterschool tutoring under SES. The not-for-profit organization had heard complaints from parents in the program, did some investigating, and decided that it wanted to get involved to make sure that the program was playing out as intended. It got the state and RCPS superintendents to support its involvement in the process. But tensions mounted as the organization urged RCPS to make changes that it lacked the authority (under federal law) to undertake.

Soon after the steering committee was formed in 2012, the state received a waiver from the federal government, giving it the authority to terminate SES and redesign and newly regulate extended learning programs and districts increased authority to design tutoring programs based on their own specifications and identified student needs. After receiving the waiver, RCPS immediately began a two-phase process of redesigning its Title I–funded tutoring programs. The task of the steering committee became to guide this. The committee members represented a number of stakeholders across the city, including community and faith-based organizations, neighborhood centers, parents, tutoring providers, and foundations, as well as several departments within the school district.

Becoming Consumers and Producers of Data in Order to Make Informed and Collaborative Program Changes

The RCPS Office of Extended Learning Opportunities frequently drew on research long before the district received a waiver, but it had limited flexibility to implement program changes in SES based on this research. This did not stop it from engaging in multiple forms of data collection around best practices and implementation research, which set a good foundation of research-to-practice once it came time to redesign its Title I–funded tutoring programs. In particular, RCPS drew on three types of research in its redesign process:

- District-generated data from parent, provider, and school-level staff surveys, as well as monitoring forms for principal and community volunteer walk-through observations of tutoring sessions.[3]
- Evaluation research from a longitudinal mixed-method study of SES in the district from 2006 to the present. This included qualitative data on the nature of the instructional setting, characteristics of tutoring formats that either facilitate or impede quality instruction, and the level of access to quality instruction for students with disabilities and English language learners, as well as quantitative data on the impact of various providers on student test scores, provider hourly rates, and hours attended. RCPS also took advantage of the district research-to-practice cooperative facilitated by this study, participating in webinars around common challenges and reaching out to another district faced with a postwaiver redesign of tutoring programs.
- More research around quality afterschool programming and digital learning. This research team assisted in providing RCPS with a collection of current, relevant, and accessible articles and reports from the broader research field as it made decisions. The district's ELO director often consulted the research base while implementing SES and drew heavily on it while redesigning the tutoring program. She developed an "article review form" for steering committee members to fill out as they read through a packet of articles on tutoring programs. She also attended national conferences on improving local systems to coordinate afterschool programs.

Building on the research and data it gathered, RCPS redesigned its federally funded tutoring program in two phases. The first phase was essentially a transition, due to the short time (two months) between receiving the waiver and the start of the school year. It was similar to SES in that various outside providers managed the logistics of tutoring but with far more regulation and input from the district.

The second phase entailed a plan to reorganize and align ELOs across the district.

With RCPS, we found ourselves examining a district in the brackish waters between two very different policy contexts: a market-based federal policy limiting districts' ability to make vendors accountable for delivering opportunities to learn (SES) and a federal policy allowing districts and states flexibility in designing how they engage with vendors and making them accountable (NCLB waiver). We are able to examine RCPS's efforts to create transparency and dialogue within each of these different policy contexts. In the example of RCPS, the efforts made possible through the flexibility of waivers strengthened vendor accountability.

Within the policy context of greater leverage and flexibility, RCPS put specific requirements into the contracts with tutoring vendors that were based in both the research and feedback from the many stakeholders represented on the steering committee.[4] For example:

- *Dosage.* The data from our study, as well as other research on out-of-school time tutoring, indicate a threshold of approximately forty hours before students start to see positive impacts on test scores. Therefore, RCPS requires that providers offer a minimum of forty-five hours of instruction to students at a maximum hourly rate of $35 per hour. This represented a $40 decrease in hourly rates for the district's primary digital tutoring vendor.
- *Class size.* Tutor-to-student ratios cannot be larger than 1:5.
- *Curriculum.* All providers must use curriculum explicitly aligned to that of the day school.
- *Transparency.* To allow for greater transparency, digital tutoring can only take place in school settings or online where RCPS can observe "virtually," and monitoring is done by school staff, the ELO Office, and the school improvement team.
- *Tutor capacity.* Providers must use certified teachers as tutors, and, in the case of digital education, these tutors must have live interaction with students during the session.

- *Access.* All providers must offer services to students with disabilities and English language learners.

As expected, there was pushback from providers, who told the district they could not provide tutoring services for a lower hourly rate. The district administrator responded by showing data from our study on the comparatively lower hourly rates charged in other districts in the study and by trying to work collaboratively with the providers to ease the transition and facilitate design changes. For example, she arranged for the district food service to provide snacks for students in school settings and waived the cost of renting RCPS classrooms for tutoring sessions.

Accountability Changes and Digital Vendors

These program changes had specific impacts on vendors of digital tutoring. For one, it cut their hourly rates by more than half by doubling the number of instructional hours students received. In addition, the district required digital vendors to provide services in school settings to better facilitate monitoring. This proved difficult for the largest digital providers in the district, and in the first year of this redesigned program they continued to provide services in students' homes.

The district also restructured its accountability requirements for digital providers to increase transparency of the instructional setting. In particular, in order to remain consistent with the monitoring requirements of the school-based providers, the district asked that the primary in-home, online vendor provide the district with five recorded tutoring sessions of students from the district.

Evaluation is a critical part of how a district like River City makes decisions about improving instruction and, ultimately, how it keeps vendors accountable for the goods and services they promise. The RCPS ELO office worked with our research team to develop monitoring forms for its school-level staff to use in evaluating the quality of digital tutoring programs. For example, the district initiated two waves of monitoring sessions in the first year of implementation so that steering committee members could "walk through" tutoring sessions using a simple evaluation tool the district developed with our assistance. The ELO office then compiled the data and sent it back to steering committee members and school and vendor administrators. RCPS envisioned this tool less as an evaluation instrument and more to facilitate discussion among the schools and vendors about program expectations and challenges. In addition to this tool, RCPS sends out surveys to school-level staff and vendors about program satisfaction and areas of improvement. It also holds an open house where teachers and parents can "walk through" and visit any tutoring session and ask questions of coordinators and vendors.

Once given the flexibility and leverage through changes in federal policy, RCPS used evidence from its own work inside the district, the research base on quality tutoring, and feedback from multiple stakeholders to make meaningful changes toward increasing learning opportunities for its low-income students. Specifically, it made efforts to improve tutoring curriculum and instruction, wrote these changes into the contracts it signs with vendors, and created monitoring tools to facilitate accountability and transparency, including in the digital context.

BLENDED ACADEMY: STRUCTURING DOWNSTREAM DIALOGUE AROUND ACCOUNTABILITY

Leveraging changes in federal policy is one way to push for greater transparency and accountability in digital education. But in large part this depends on upstream changes. Another way is to build a case for change from the ground up by structuring a dialogue whereby the experiences of students and teachers in a digital school inform downstream discussions, where contract decisions are made. What follows is a story about how educators, students, and researchers at Blended Academy tried to bring to the fore issues about curriculum, instruction, and assessment that weren't visible to those in charge of the digital curriculum contract.

In BA's blueprint, the founders identified a multileveled dialogue as a key component of the school's success. This was the impetus behind BA's decision to collaborate with university faculty and graduate students in an evaluation of school's progress, the hope being that school and community dialogue on blended learning would support strategic improvements in ways that benefited students academically, socially, and emotionally.

One of BA's initial steering committee members was a former *New York Times* journalist who was working as a journalism professor. The plan, first hatched in a steering committee meeting and then approved by its members, was to have his journalism students write documentaries on students' experiences at BA that the BA students would then edit for language arts credit. From this assignment the journalism students would gain valuable experience on the challenges of reporting on and in public schools. Further, the documentaries would be shared with community and staff to elicit feedback on the school's design. In this way, a dialogue on learning was to be intertwined among the research, the school, and the university.

Partly in response to start-up funding pressures, in the summer before BA opened, the school's governance shifted. A principal was hired and a new governing board was formed, this one made up largely of influential members of the local and national charter school movement. The school needed money, and it hoped that these individuals could help generate revenue. With this, the governance conversation around BA shifted somewhat to focus on the arguments heard in the national dialogue around blended learning and charter schools. There was a lot of talk about scalability and profitability. Angel investors were keen on making sure that they got their money's worth. As the financial pressure to keep the school open and potentially bring it to scale consumed more of the board's time, other key aspects of the dialogue—the quality of learning, accessibility for low-income students, and support for teaching staff—became secondary, both in terms of priority and in terms of the authority of those involved in the conversation. Part of that shift involved appointing university faculty to oversee research on the program. The charge to the research team was to conduct an evaluation of the school that would show its impact, or lack thereof, which would be key to gaining more funding.

Engaging with Research and Prompting a Dialogue

The new governance board also decided that it needed a research policy so that it could better manage the information about the school that was shared with the broader public. These decisions came on the heels of a widely released report by the Education Policy Center that looked at the implementation and impact of one prominent online school company, K12 Inc., and concluded that online learning was far from a silver bullet. According to the report, online learning without face-to-face teacher interaction did little to improve students' learning opportunities. The school's founder saw this as a highly damaging report to the idea of blended learning, and the board agreed that evidence was needed that would distance the program (both in kind and in effects) from the program that had not worked. A school of education faculty member who had served on the original steering committee joined with two other researchers to design a preliminary research strategy aimed at understanding the intervention. The strategy employed interviews, focus groups, observations, and survey data to better understand (1) which students selected to attend BA and why, (2) teaching practices (both designed and enacted), and (3) students' exposure to the curriculum, including the content of the curriculum and opportunities to learn.

BA's founder developed a rationale for the research in her blueprint for the school and created a structure (university-based partnership) to support the research. The research team took this vision and translated it into an action plan that was reviewed with staff and modified based on some of their suggestions. Individual teachers then worked with graduate students to build research tools and questions (e.g., student perceptions) relevant to instructional issues emerging in their own classrooms. There wasn't a research budget yet, but school leaders supported the idea and agreed to fund graduate students to assist faculty in the research design and collection of data.

As the research team worked on its design, one fact became very clear: the national conversation on blended learning that was influencing BA's leadership offered little by way of practical tools to conduct research in nontraditional school settings. The handful of studies on blended learning contained few concrete means for capturing the nuances of BA's instructional model. Most of the surveys out there were geared for brick-and-mortar schools and offered only a very partial view on what they were doing. The digital school wanted very much to leverage and be part of a larger conversation on blended learning. However, that dialogue wasn't well formed yet. There was little research to draw on, and there were even fewer "tools" (e.g., surveys) that could be adapted for use.

So the research team decided that it would help structure and bring resources to the dialogue by focusing on the issues that had not yet garnered much attention. Specifically, the team wanted to understand digital schools from the perspective of those teaching and learning in them and use those perspectives to build a model for beginning to understand effects. Propelled by insights from watching students use the digital curriculum and talking to teachers and students about their experiences, the team expanded the research focus to include greater and deeper attention to the quality of the digital curriculum and its effects on instruction and assessment—critical pieces taken for granted in the founder's initial research design.

Researchers conducted interviews with the school staff soon after students started attending BA, with the purpose of understanding the expectations that teachers brought to the school, how they viewed their roles and their past experiences. After several weeks, teachers were overwhelmed with the amount of work and with a disintegrating model that wasn't working as anticipated. At this point, and beyond, it became more difficult to schedule times to talk with teachers. Still, the teachers were open to observation, welcoming the researchers into their classes weekly. Usually, the teachers wanted to chat about their lessons after the observation, when there was time, either asking for thoughts and suggestions or wanting to debrief or explain some of their strategies. The teachers seemed eager to discuss what they had discovered about teaching in a digital school in a confidential space, and the staff meetings did not yet provide that setting.

As the year progressed, interviews and casual conversations with teachers exhibited increasing discontent. Teachers complained about issues such as professional development, other teachers' discipline practices, and/or the curriculum. Their initial optimism for "the textbook" (Pyramid) plummeted, and the digital curriculum became viewed primarily as an obstacle to powerful teaching. Interestingly, the board, however, was not questioning if the curriculum was working but, rather, was more focused on building a transactional model, asking, "What is the market for what we are doing and how can we leverage and control information about the school in that market?" There was no structure or process in place for bringing together these two levels of dialogue. There were, however, points in the process when various staff members tried to do so. For example, the principal raised the point at one board meeting that the curriculum demanded some tweaking of the teacher evaluation protocol. The board's response was that issues of teacher evaluation were outside of the realm of the contract, even though the board would need to sign off on it. This presented school leadership with a dilemma: the contract for the curriculum and the curriculum itself set standards for what teachers were expected to do; therefore, the limitations of the curriculum needed to be acknowledged and discussed in order for and fair and appropriate teacher evaluations protocol to be developed.

Tracking Teachers' Experiences

By the middle of the school year, BA teachers had begun to address and try to compensate for weaknesses in the digital curriculum. A primary challenge facing teachers was to make the curriculum more accessible for students who lacked the skill sets for the level in which they were placed. Another challenge facing teachers was finding a way to communicate and learn from each others' experiences given the lack of professional development, the hectic schedule, and the school's fast start-up. School leaders used group e-mails to communicate with teachers. These ad-hoc and structured communications shared with researchers became an important window into teachers' concerns about the curriculum, helping researchers track and better understand teachers' agitation with otherwise opaque aspects of the program, particularly the online curriculum. Teachers' use of technology (e-mail, Google docs) to identify shared concerns with the curriculum moved the "what works?" dialogue forward.

The e-mails capture the teachers' growing agitation with the curriculum. At the beginning of the year, reflecting national public conversation, they referred to the Pyramid curriculum as *high-tech, blended,* and *differentiated.* By the middle of the year, reference to the technology moved to the background. In e-mails to the principal and to one another, teachers voiced concerns with managing student behavior, tracking student progress, developing student accountability and personal responsibility, and fostering school pride and independence. While at the beginning of the year the teachers discussed Pyramid as if it were something new and different that they felt had the potential to alter their teaching, by the middle of the year it became simply "the textbook"—something the teachers used for basic content but not for their main lessons. Discussion about instruction moved from being centered on Pyramid to being centered on teacher-created resources. In these and other ways, teachers formed a counternarrative to the problems generated by the digital curriculum. Put differently, these e-mail conversations created some space in which teachers could think about what they could do to create similar spaces for students (to react to curriculum) in the context of classroom assignments.

By the middle to end of the school year, it became very apparent to researchers that pressures and confusion on the part of teachers was figuring centrally in students' experiences of the BA program. Teachers were worried for students—for their safety, whether they were learning, their sense of connectedness to school—and talked about these concerns in e-mails, interviews, and professional development sessions.

Bringing Students into the Dialogue

At the beginning of the year, researchers relied on several student focus groups that centered on students' previous schooling experiences, early impressions of BA, and goals. Some students were eager to speak openly with the researchers, while others shared responses reluctantly, giving mostly short answers with long periods of silence and often only responding if directly addressed. In several cases, students began asking the researchers for connections to opportunities that they weren't receiving at the school, including internships, high school exchange programs, and athletics.

In order to build on that rapport, researchers discussed the possibility of increasing their participation in the school community by acting as teaching assistants and/or tutors during their time on-site. The research team, administrators, and teachers all seemed to like the idea and cleared researchers to interact more directly with students. However, the researchers found that, unlike in their previous experiences working in nonblended high school classrooms, they had trouble figuring out what each student was supposed to be doing and what productive role they could play in supporting students' interactions with the digital curriculum. Because each student could be working on something different, it was almost impossible to be prepared to tutor or assist a student in progressing through the Pyramid curriculum. If, for example, a student went to an individual teacher for help, the tutor couldn't see what the student was looking at without invading the privacy of their home screen. Additionally, because of the shifting nature of classroom procedures and norms, it was necessary for researchers to constantly check in with teachers to make sure that they were helping students with the correct lesson in the correct way. In order to diminish any instructional intrusion on already-burdened teachers, the researchers resumed the role of passive observers.

But as access to student experiences continued to be a challenge throughout the first semester, one researcher, a former high school English teacher, discussed the possibility of collaborating on a project with a teacher. In building a classroom community and culture around the project, the researcher, teacher, and students began each session with check-ins, where they would share their highs and lows of the week and what they were looking forward to. The researcher found that from the first project session, when they began that practice, students responded strongly to what seemed like a novel opportunity for them to talk about themselves and their lives within BA. Many students immediately started sharing their personal experiences with the group, ranging from frustration with discipline policies at the school to arguments that they had with their parents or excitement over getting a new skateboard that week. Some students were reluctant to share and, when probed for feedback about their hesitation, bluntly stated that they questioned the value of taking time to talk about themselves when so many of them were behind in the digital curriculum.

These comments opened up rich but sometimes tense dialogue among students about whether or not it was worth building community at BA, how many of them would actually work on the digital curriculum in that time if they weren't participating in the project, and whether the curriculum felt like a privilege or a waste of time to them.

Momentum Behind Teacher Dialogue Increases

There was now a very real, honest dialogue about students' experiences starting to build among a researcher, a teacher, and the students. And there was also an active and increasingly energized dialogue among teachers in meetings and via e-mail around the problems of the digital curriculum. In one professional development meeting, the teachers discussed the very real consequences of using Pyramid for high-stakes testing. Teacher and administrators alike felt that Pyramid fell short on preparing students for these tests, which would have negative consequences for the school. Teachers expressed concern that Pyramid was not well-aligned with standards in content or rigor and that using it would result in poor test scores for students and, consequently, problems for the school. And both teachers and administrators felt that although Pyramid required a score of 80 percent to demonstrate mastery and the state tests only require that students score 67 percent to be designated "proficient," students would still score "below proficient" on the state tests due to this misalignment.

Similarly, the teachers discussed the issues surrounding the effects of offering a wide range of math courses. Many students were placed into Pyramid's remedial "general math" and, as a consequence of the course structure, were moving at the same pace as students in grade-level and higher-level math courses. Thus, there were a lot of students who were not working on grade level and not being prepared for state testing. Teachers and administrators again worried that this would reflect poorly on the school.

In addition to these concerns, teachers also grew increasingly concerned about the connection between Pyramid and their employee evaluations. In one professional development discussion a teacher asked, "We're supposed to be an individualized school, but what does that look like in an evaluation rubric?" This led to a lengthy discussion about the insufficient nature of Pyramid and the anxiety teachers felt about being evaluated in relation to students' progress through Pyramid. During this conversation, it was evident that teachers questioned not only how they would be evaluated but also what their role was expected to be in relation to Pyramid. As highlighted in the excerpt at the beginning of this chapter, one teacher wondered, "Are we expecting teachers to rely on Pyramid for the presentation of content? Or are we saying that the teachers are responsible?" In response, an administrator replied, "We need to curate Pyramid. Sometimes Pyramid isn't going to be sufficient," clarifying that when it comes to evaluation, "if you're just looking at Pyramid, you're evaluating Pyramid, not the teacher."

Gaps in Governance Dialogue

These important issues raised by both students and teachers never made it into the dialogue taking place at the board level, where the decision to continue or terminate teacher contracts ultimately would be made. This governance dialogue framed stakes in terms of the school's ability to go to scale (be replicated) and thereby reduce costs.

In board-level dialogue there was heavy emphasis on gaining external support in terms of more funding, maintaining cost efficiencies, and managing public opinion of the new school—which the board hoped to scale-up with the opening of many more schools within a few years. Inside the school and in the exchanges within and across students and staff, there continued to be active chronicling of the very real limitations of the digital curriculum that the school was leasing. Unlike struggles over transparency and accountability in River City, the downstream dialogue on the limitations of Pyramid curriculum at Blended Academy was conducted outside of formal policy channels. The board didn't interact with teachers and students beyond a few invited presentations where teachers would present on topics like the math curriculum (these presentations were early in the year, though, before the staff started being more critical of Pyramid).

Despite teachers' very prominent roles as enactors and translators of the Pyramid curriculum and their persistent efforts to alert superiors to the limits of the curriculum, they had very little power over continuation of the contract. Without regular interaction with the board or a forum for voicing concerns around contracted curriculum, the substantive barriers in students' opportunities to learn in the digital school didn't get attention from the board. They remained downstream issues—real, significant, but disconnected from policy conversations driving the school.

What will become of Blended Academy as an experiment in cutting-edge blended learning high schools is unclear. Whatever the future holds for BA, certain conditions for continued dialogue have been set. The ability and efforts of teachers to critique and respond to the contracted curriculum has focused a more public lens on the quality of contracted digital education. With the help of researchers, teachers resisted the idea suggested by one superior that "curriculum issues are teacher issues, not governance issues" and pushed public awareness of the importance of the quality of digital curriculum into more public arenas (professional development, documentation of practice by third parties) and into more experimental spaces (classroom assignments, student learning, student work). Teachers' efforts augmented and created space for some students to articulate concerns about the curriculum and challenge the belief that any digital curriculum is preferable to the textbook curriculum. In the end, what matters most is that educators looking to BA as a model for replication see blended learning through an honest lens—one that prioritizes lived experiences over outside pressures to model success and scalability. Dialogue around curriculum, instruction, and assessment in digital education needs to incorporate these kinds of authentic, local, lived experiences of those participating in it. As one student commented during a reflective exercise:

> I would like to change the way people look at my community. How people think of it as a place with ghettoes and violence. Even though there is ghettos and violence, it is not that bad. Yes, I do hear police all the time, yes there have been fights and yes it gets on my nerves, but that isn't all there is to it [my community]. There isn't violence all the time. It is a very lovely place. My community has tons of graffiti and you can always smell smoke from someone's kitchen or their family barbecue. My community is also loud. It is always filled with music or people arguing. But the thing I love the most about my community are the people, the relationships, with everyone and how everyone is close and how everyone gossips with one another, everyone in a way confides in one another, whether it is asking for milk, money or advice.

The BA story is really about structuring the dialogue, determining what the dialogue is about (e.g., technical issues or instructional issues), who gets to decide what it is about, and who is actually involved, including students. The central question—What is worth fighting for in a digital school?—developed through small actions and dialogue among teachers and students teaching and learning inside the school. By moving the dialogue away from the transactional issues (cost efficiencies, school management) and expanding exploration of students' and teachers' experiences of the school and the effects of outside forces such as poverty, the school and the researchers gained valuable insights on students' experiences with the curriculum and their needs that the curriculum was not addressing. The hope is that these perspectives will inform the broader conversation around what is worth fighting for at BA and strategies for reaching these goals.

ACCELERATED BLENDED LEARNING:
ENGAGING IN SELF-REFLEXIVE DIALOGUE
WITH ALL STAKEHOLDERS

Accelerated Blended Learning has a well-developed curriculum that is aligned and assessed in varied ways and created and delivered by certified teachers with experience in digital education. Yet, there is a persistent gap in how it serves low-income students within its programs, one consistent with historic and national trends in gifted education.[5] Therefore, ABL is now engaged in a long, challenging dialogue that is less about increasing the program's already considerable transparency and more about increasing its accountability to issues of access for low-income students.

Underrepresentation is not a new issue in gifted education. Efforts to better represent particular student populations, namely students of color from such historically underrepresented groups as bilingual students, low-income students, and students with disabilities, date back to the 1970s.[6] Ultimately, addressing these underrepresentations in gifted programs in general, and ABL in particular, comes down to identification and programming.[7] Since the districts that contracts with ABL determines the identification process for gifted students, ABL is in a self-initiated, self-reflexive process of examining what about their course structure or programming might also lead to lower enrollment of low-income students.

Ten years ago ABL began a conversation within its own program and with its partners around the limitations of the current identification system, but the effort was met with resistance, somewhat on the part of the program's own instructional staff at the time who were tied to traditional ways of defining and assessing giftedness. In addition, ABL has its hands tied in terms of identification of students eligible for gifted programming since this is done at the school and district levels. But ABL's leaders realize that other factors play into the program's low enrollment of students from low-income communities. As the program director explains, "The challenging questions are about assessing and getting [low-income] students into gifted programs, and then now that we have them in the program what does that mean for the curriculum and the strategies, what happens next so that the conversation isn't just about identification?" And this is where ABL stands now. They are engaged in a dialogue around how to better support and retain low-income students in their blended courses, a discussion that has a number of implications in the digital environment. Again, as the director said, "The idea that giftedness is in all populations has always been there, it is in the implementation and actuality of things that it can fall apart."[8] In essence, ABL is engaged in a dialogue with stakeholders to understand how "implementation and actuality" create such a challenge to making quality blended learning accessible to gifted low-income students and students of color.

What ABL Learned from Dialogue with Stakeholders

As part of the process to increase access to its programs, ABL not only engaged its own program-level data on enrollment and student satisfaction relative to low-income students, but it also held multiple listening sessions around the state with school- and district-level administrators. Although still very much in the middle of the dialogue, some critical questions and themes have emerged through these conversations about the challenges facing gifted students from low-income families.

- *Cost of tuition.* ABL cannot determine eligibility for its programs, but it can determine the pricing structure. A concern for some schools with high numbers of low-income students is being able to pay tuition. To address this, ABL applied for and received grants from the state department of instruction to offset a large discount on tuition that students eligible for free and reduced-price lunch receive. The tuition is $25 per student per quarter instead of $195 or $250. They essentially have eliminated the cost barrier to enrolling low-income students and in fact have given schools incentive to include a greater proportion of low-income students among their ABL enrollees.

- *Access to computers.* Low-income families tend to not have regular access to the Internet, making it difficult for students to complete online coursework at home. Typically ABL students spend 12–15 hours per week on the course, with only 5 or so of the hours using computers at school. To complicate matters, students from larger urban schools may not have regular access to computers, even at school. Low-income students are thus at a disadvantage with having less time to work online. This is a larger structural challenge, but ABL is examining the possibility of either making program changes around the amount of time required on courses or somehow assisting schools in acquiring additional hardware for student work.

- *Foundational skills.* Various school-level stakeholders expressed concern that students coming from schools serving large numbers of low-income students seem to need more foundational technical skills on using the Internet and navigating an online platform. As a result, ABL went back to the schools and districts to ask for feedback on how to best address the need for additional technical skills and then suggested an ABL 101 course to offer students as an introduction to and practice in navigating the platform and the expectations they will use for writing and reading assignments. The ABL 101 course also provides students new to ABL an opportunity for interacting with other ABL students and teachers.

- *Content of the courses.* Feedback from some district stakeholders, as well as the research base, suggested that the content of courses and the nature of interactions between students and teachers might improve to become a more culturally responsive learning environment for all students. In other words, students from all kinds of socioeconomic backgrounds must feel that their own life experiences and contexts are represented and respected in the ABL coursework. As a step toward addressing cultural relevancy in the curriculum, ABL has recently included in summer staff trainings topics such as how to facilitate discussion around challenging issues in diverse classrooms.

- *School-level support.* The lower tuition ABL offers for students who are eligible for free and reduced-price lunch doesn't help when the school-level counselor is not able to adequately support additional kids. An early attempt to address this problem was a grant-funded ABL initiative designed to fund counselors in urban schools in the hope that they would identify more low-income students and students of color for ABL enrollment. But while the counselors were on board with the idea, and they were able to identify more gifted students, they did not have the time to support these students. As a step toward addressing this lack of school-level capacity, ABL 101 aimed at decreasing the need for scaffolding on the part of school counselors by offering students more preparation and foundation for navigating the online course.

Through this dialogue with various stakeholders, ABL is hoping to craft a coherent set of strategies to make its digital courses more accessible to students from low-income settings. A number of possible variables contribute to how ABL is able to engage in the types of dialogue that are putting them on the path to increasing access to its blended courses for low-income students.

- *Responsibility to and relationship with stakeholders including teachers, students, community,* depend on school-level decisions on enrollment, so the organization and instructional design needs to be responsive or otherwise ABL will not get contracts. Therefore, the structure and avenues for dialogue, especially through relationships, are preexisting and well-established.
- *High-capacity administrative and instructional staff.* ABL rely on administrators and staff who know education and have engaged in lots of thought and discussion about instruction, access, and opportunities to learn.
- *Flexibility.* ABL is not locked into either a purchased curriculum or a static, top-down curriculum of its own. Courses, their

design, and content are intended to be dynamic, and instructors are encouraged to make changes (and compensated for doing so) to the courses from year to year, including to course structures and content that may better serve low-income students.

Ultimately, we aren't saying that ABL is a model that, if applied to all digital education, would somehow fix it. It simply illustrates, as all the examples do in this chapter, how people in particular contexts carve out and structure dialogue around increasing opportunities to learn in a system of digital education.

CRITICAL QUESTIONS AND POTENTIAL SOLUTIONS

Greater transparency around and attention to the role of the teacher, the roles of data and assessments, and the nature of curriculum and what we assume is worth knowing are exactly where the dialogue must start if we are to get any closer to holding vendors and policy makers accountable for whether digital education improves teaching and learning for students living in high-poverty settings. Districts and schools need tools for engaging in this dialogue. Figure I.1 not only frames our own analysis of digital education around the three critical areas of curriculum, assessment, and data/assessment, but it offers a tool to help districts and schools visualize how decisions made by vendors of digital education products and services have real impact on learning opportunities for their students.

This systematic way of seeing digital education helps districts match the characteristics of various types of digital education platforms to particular student needs. For instance, synchronous programs with a live instructor that drives instruction (situated in quadrant A in figure 6.2) may work better for students with particular disabilities who need frequent adaptations and greater scaffolding for assignments. Yet, software-driven asynchronous programs (situated in quadrant B in figure 6.2) may be a better match for migrant students that frequently come in and out of a district and may not have regular access to the Internet.

FIGURE 6.2   Applied examples: critical decisions toward quality and access in contracting for digital education

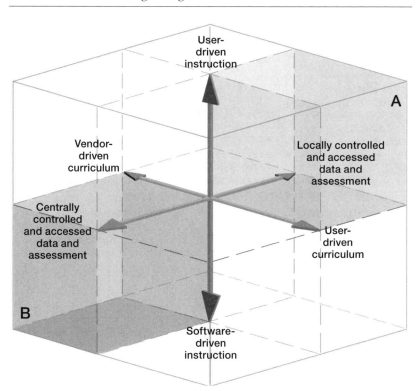

The figure also can guide districts in designing ways to best monitor and evaluate vendor programs. Imagine districts coming up with a model for monitoring the types of platforms that fall within a certain quadrant in figure 6.2. For example, in establishing ways to do walk-through monitoring of tutoring sessions, district contracts with vendors in quadrant B (such as Project Achieve from chapter 5) might include provisions to allow for home visits of students and for districts to obtain a copy of the software program used to drive instruction, as well as access to the assessment data. Figure 6.3 includes sample questions districts might ask digital education vendors in the contracting process. These are based on the concepts framed in figure I.1

FIGURE 6.3   Sample questions for policy makers, administrators, and educators to ask digital education vendors in the contracting process

Curriculum	Instruction	Data and assessment
▪ Who developed the curriculum? ▪ To what extent can it be adapted and by whom (e.g., artificial intelligence in software vs. a live teacher)? ▪ What is the curriculum based on or aligned to and how is this measured? ▪ What kind of access to "see" the curriculum in use?	▪ Who/What drives or progresses instruction (e.g., manages pace, assigns tasks, assesses understanding, responds to student questions)—an instructor or software? ▪ How is instruction adapted to students' diverse needs? ▪ How would district staff observe or monitor instruction?	▪ Who/What has access to both formative and summative assessment data? ▪ Who/What decides what data should be included in measures of student learning and teacher evaluation? ▪ What checks are in place to ensure validity and reliability, and does the user have a role in this process? ▪ Who determines how data is shared (both internally and publically) and with whom?

and offer specific examples of questions to guide districts and users when determining digital education contracts.

Once districts and schools gain greater transparency into the nature of contracted digital education, that knowledge must be leveraged to increase access to quality digital programming for all students. Shifting the upstream current is critical. We must press on policy to discipline the market where it seems to be working against the needs of low-income students and press on the market to nudge policy where it creates barriers to this work. But these upstream endeavors will not occur absent upstream and downstream dialogue on instructional issues.

A midlevel administrator in River City dared to demand that online and other providers agree to minimum standards of transparency and accountability as a condition of receiving public dollars. The role of the policy in this dialogue ultimately was to establish these standards based on the best evidence available and to use whatever authority within reach to enforce them. As a consequence of this dialogue and action, the issue of who is teaching these children and under what conditions became part of the contract between the district and the vendor, as did the quality of the curriculum. The district wanted to know what students are being taught and what assurance they had that content is somewhat aligned to the content for which they are responsible and to which students will be held accountable.

Blended Academy staff, graduate students, and university personnel dared to ask, "What is the quality of the data we are getting in this supposed high-tech environment?" Behind the glitz and promises, are the data teachers are being asked to work with any better than the data in regular public schools, schools that big software companies characterize as "backward"? With this question the limits of the curriculum vendor became obvious, and the discussion about what kind of data mattered to this school, given its vision, was ignited.

In the case of Accelerated Blended Learning, a not-for-profit vendor forged a different path and created high-quality learning opportunities that depended on technology for activation. Meaningful dialogue provided the foundation for and built a highly functioning curriculum. Technology became a means through which public school students with a passion for civics or problem solving or literature could dig much deeper into a content area. ABL dared to ask hard and difficult questions of its own program, pushing to increase access to its programs regardless of students' socioeconomic backgrounds. These examples illustrate how productive dialogue can be initiated locally, where digital education comes downstream.[9] But it can't stop there.

These stakeholders worked in specific ways to push forward the conversation around equity and quality in digital education (see figure 6.1). Each was successful to some degree. However, at the point where we left them, each community had reached a critical bend in the river, where the next steps appeared unclear and the obstacles significant. Looking toward and drawing from these cases, we turn to areas critical in moving to the next level of dialogue around increasing opportunities to learn in digital education.

CHAPTER 7

Equal Scrutiny

Digital Education and the Struggle for Equity, Quality, and Accountability

OVER THE COURSE of this book, we have journeyed into the everyday work of digital education—beyond the boundaries of what is typically advertised on the web or broadly mapped in school or company descriptions. The kinds of digital education we study here—digital courses, digital schools, digital tutoring—are characteristic of a surge in online schooling and portend a larger groundswell that is changing the foundation of schooling and the governance of public schooling in the United States and abroad.

"Equal scrutiny," as the title of this book urges, is one way to think differently about the challenge of accountability in digital education. We need to ask not only how public schools can use digital education to improve the quality of instruction but also what role, if any, digital education serves in the broader agenda to create more equitable access to high-quality instruction in our schools and communities. We need answers to the big question: How can we influence upstream forces—both industry and policy—to invest (figuratively and literally) in digital education in ways that value *both* equity and quality? We also need answers to the related questions, such as, What are the critical leverage points in curriculum, instruction, and assessment that move us closer toward this goal?

In this closing chapter we discuss why equal scrutiny of access and quality, as well as public and private actions, is particularly important now and what stakeholders involved in digital education, as well as working actively on issues of equality and opportunity, can do to make changes.

WHAT HANGS IN THE BALANCE?

The landscape of private engagement in public education has shifted. Both in the United States and abroad there exists a movement to reorient education policy and practice around the theoretical principles of the marketplace. The bigger idea driving this trend is the premise that the market can provide more efficient and innovative solutions to pressing social problems than government bureaucracies can, and therefore governments increasingly should contract for or outsource what they typically have paid public employees to do. The press to increase the role of nongovernment actors in publicly funded programs is rapidly expanding in scope, cutting across different levels of schooling (from pre-K to higher education) and segments of society (public health, defense, transportation), and has quickly become a global phenomenon.

Although outside contracting has a long history in the U.S. education system, public schools are being transformed by market-based reforms and the dramatic shift in the role of outside vendors. Public agencies long have contracted out for operational services, such as transportation and food service, as well as instructional services for special populations, such as incarcerated youth, students with severe physical or mental disabilities, and for the scoring and reporting of test score data. But in recent decades the breadth and depth of outside agencies' engagement and the explicit purposes of this engagement have changed in ways that increase the influence of these organizations on the core functions of public schools: teaching and learning.

Contracting for instructional services in public schools is exploding at the very same time that the poverty rates of school-age children are increasing, leaving public schools hanging in the balance. The settings in which these contracts are being established has shifted, with increasing numbers of students in public schools living in poverty. Therefore, the role of public schools in ensuring high-quality and equitable learning opportunities for *all* students is becoming even more critical. There are more school-aged children living in poverty than there were a decade ago and more children with at least one parent unemployed. Poverty creates significant barriers to school completion. African Americans and Latinos have higher proportions of families with school-aged children living in poverty than do whites and Asian Americans. Public schools are still segregated by race and by income. Disparities in education outcomes between students from low- and high-income settings persist, as does the unequal distribution of resources.[1]

These disparities are heightened in light of evidence that there is an increased level of investment needed by districts in order to meet the needs of high-poverty students. Yet few states or districts have formulas that come anywhere close to making up the difference. With budget cuts in school funding and programs, wealthier parents have worked to supplement public school budgets through individual donations channeled through not-for-profit organizations. These donations have helped buffer public schools in wealthier communities from budget cuts, further increasing the resource disparities within public school systems between the haves and have-nots. These are the political and economic spaces into which digital education has entered and thrived. The rise in contracting, as part of a larger surge in austerity measures for critical social programs, comes at a time when poverty is hurting more and more children and their life chances. It increases the stakes of ensuring that the core objectives of public education—equity, excellence, democratic participation—are met.

PROFIT OR EQUITY? COMPETING INTERESTS IN CONTRACTING FOR DIGITAL EDUCATION

Contracting for instructional services such as digital courses, schools, and tutoring illustrates the central tension within the movement to privatize, contract out, and marketize public schools—a tension between profit and equity. Behind this tension is the expense of developing, delivering, and assessing quality digital education, as well as bringing it to scale. It takes time, money, skills, and other resources. Who will bear the considerable expense of bringing quality digital education to kids from low-income families who, unlike middle- and upper-middle-income families, cannot bear that cost themselves? In other words, who will bear the cost and responsibility of ensuring quality and equity in digital education?

The equity imperative involves a conscious effort to compensate for and address the fact that those with economic privilege tend to also have technological privilege. This redistribution of resources— where those who have less get more—is a hard case to make to an industry for which the ultimate goal, naturally, is making money. When there is more government money for social programs, the case is easier to make, because companies can market themselves to the poor. When government resources are tight, companies want to make as much money as they can by selling more and reducing costs, and this reduces incentives for for-profit companies to develop and distribute high-quality products for historically disadvantaged and culturally marginalized children. High-quality digital education for these groups costs industries money when the government isn't paying. It costs companies money to hire a live tutor who can work specifically with English language learners. It costs companies money to provide students who don't have Internet access with a card that enables access, instead of expecting students to go to their nearest McDonalds for Internet access. In this context, the gap between talk and action can be very wide. It is one thing to say that the best of your digital courseware will be available to public school students, regardless of cost; it is quite another thing to take the specific actions to make this possible in one community, much less nationally. So, there is a tension here that puts high-poverty students at a distinct disadvantage when it comes to high-quality digital education driven by investor activity.

CHANGING CURRENTS THROUGH
STRUCTURED DIALOGUE

But how do stakeholders in both the downstream (teachers, parents, students) and upstream (policy makers, concerned vendors) currents of digital education mitigate this tension to increase opportunities to learn for low-income students? By closely studying the everyday work of digital education, we have gained a strategic vantage point for viewing and assessing the give and take, the possibilities and risks, involved in this work. Every format and every variety of digital education has its trade-offs. It is not our place to determine the right combination of these formats and varieties to address the needs of every district, school, or student; Instead, we suggest a way of conceptualizing these trade-offs as a tool for those whose place it is.

There are spectra of decisions to be made by vendors, policy makers, and educators, and, as the three cases in this book detail, these decisions matter enormously to quality and equity in digital education. We can now be more specific about defining the conversations that best open digital education to its promising future in public schools. The conversations are designed to create transparency and accountability as well as build commitment to principles of quality and equity. The traditional policy instruments of mandates, incentives, sanctions, and system overhauls are very important and potentially powerful components of the change process, but by themselves they not enough, and they are not our focus here. Instead, the driving premise of our work is that structured dialogue is a critical component of transformation in digital education, given the complex interplay of vendors, policy makers, and practitioners. The kinds of questions we ask matter; questions can sometimes be more powerful than a list of mandates or imperatives in that they create opportunities for engagement.[2] How we frame those questions is also critical. The questions that have anchored our analysis in this book are designed to be immediate and relevant to educators while identifying the larger implications for public education. Thus, we ask about curriculum, instruction, assessment, and the role of the vendor as we consider the bigger questions of what knowledge matters, what is happening to the role of the teacher, and who controls and has access to data.

If our conception of digital education fully integrated the value of equity and access, we might depict it as a figure organized around the core education dimensions of curriculum, instruction and data/assessment (see figure I.1). Each of these three axes or arenas for decision making represented in the figure is important. Along each axes there is a continuum of decisions that push us closer or further away from achieving the goal of high-quality digital education for all students. And these decisions will and should be different in different contexts, whether it is an alternative urban high school or after-school tutoring. In the same sense that education technology is not a silver bullet, there is no one, best way to do digital education. An important part of the struggle toward accountability in digital education is to ensure equal scrutiny of both government and vendor practice in these areas, which should be included in or integral to any comprehensive effort for addressing quality and equity in digital education.

What Kinds of Data and Outcomes Matter in the Digital Education Age, and Who Decides What Matters?

The whole question of data and making decisions based on data is at the forefront of policy debates. Many of the conversations are focused on how we can best nail down accurate data, explain or define the accuracy of the data, or compel educators to use the data. Beneath these questions is a larger issue that has to do with control. Much of what happens in public education in the next generation will be driven by who dictates what counts as data and who controls the data itself.

Figure I.1 gives schools, districts, and vendors a way to conceptualize this continuum of data control and access. First, on one end of the digital data continuum is data that is *centrally controlled and accessed*. In the digital tutoring example in chapter 1, Lynnette and her father ended the digital tutoring session with more issues than answers about the quality of the digital tutoring program. Her father, if you recall, sat with his daughter as she inputted answers from the worksheet into the computer. All they got back was a "Good job man!" Her father didn't know who to call once the session ended. The vendor controlled the data on when the session began and ended and, in this manner, how much the session cost the district. Across the country, students and parents, including Lynette and her father, came to meetings held by our research team seeking more access and transparency around the data they were giving and getting from digital education. They wanted data that would assist them in supporting their child in the digital education setting. At a meeting held on Mother's Day, Lynette's father asked about the math problems that he saw on the screen—where did they come from? They were different than the math problems that his daughter brought home on the worksheet in her backpack. What is the point of this instruction, he asked, if the practice tests his daughter is working on measure different math skills than the ones she is working on and accountable for in school? He and others wanted answers to questions that touched on larger collective issues. They wanted to know the selection processes behind the digital vendors offering the free instruction and how they were evaluated.

On the other end of the continuum is data that is *locally accessible and whose meaning is co-constructed*. In contrast to the example offered above, the case of Accelerated Blended Learning illustrates ways in which data can be co-constructed among the teacher, assessment systems, software, and even students, like Anthony. In the case of the blended online course in chapter 3, "URule School," the teacher assessed Anthony and his classmates based on learning goals and assigned ratings of 0–4 for their growth in particular goals on each assignment. Besides the teacher, Anthony and his school counselor have access not only to the ratings but to the comments and suggestions his teachers posted online. Teachers create the assessment and generate the formative feedback based on these assessments. Anthony has the chance to revise his work and assess his own growth on learning goals, adding to the data on his progress. Anthony also assesses other students' work as a "critical friend," offering targeted feedback through online forums on both form and substance. The work that Anthony and his teacher do around his learning goals then becomes part of a larger set of assessment data that is collected by the ABL administrators using the open-source software platform. These data are organized into areas such as "total learning targets used," "average growth," and student satisfaction and compiled into a summary report that provides assessment trends across ABL as well as individual reports for each teacher.

In the digital school story, the data generated by a centralized (and in fact imperfect and unreliable) computer program was used to penalize Justin, the boy who wanted to be a lawyer and whose struggles were interpreted by the computer as noncompletion. He had his computer taken away from him because the data from the computer identified him as failing. There are risks in assuming that digital data is good data or that digital data is open, accessible data. Anne Schneider and Helen Ingram, writing about the growing influence of research universities and think tanks with large research budgets and big complicated data sets in deciding what works in education and other aspects of public policy, have argued that broader shifts in determining "what data matter" contribute in very direct ways to whose expertise is valued in public policy decisions.[3] The emphasis on more data, faster data, and more technical data moves authority over public policy away from educators and parents and toward professionals with technical expertise to manipulate the data.[4] Building on this work, we suggest that without greater transparency and accountability, digital education can move data further out of reach of educators and parents and toward commercial vendors that have a financial interest in the data. As more data is generated by digital education, questions around the purpose of that data and who owns that data must be carefully scrutinized, particularly given that the selling of data increasingly involves vendors in other social programs, such as health care for the poor.

What Drives Instruction, and What is the Role of the Teacher?

The instructional setting and role of the teacher are also at the forefront of policy debates. Much of the current conversation seems to focus on what teachers need to know and be able to do to be effective instructors and the kinds of programs and organizational arrangements that can support teacher mastery. At the core of the conversations are debates around the role of the teacher and distribution of instructional resources.

In digital education as conceptualized in figure I.1, on one end of the instruction continuum is the expectation, reflected in the design of both software and hardware, that a *live teacher* still has primary responsibility for students' learning. In contrast, the implicit understanding on the other end of the continuum is that a digital environment can function without a teacher and should be primarily *software driven*.

In the ABL case, vendors are leveraging technology to support teachers' professional identities and capacities. The digital platform enables teachers to interact with students in ways mainly prohibited in regular classrooms without a digital component. Anthony and his fellow students in "URule School" came from different schools and different districts, but through the blended course model could interact with one another and their teacher around critical higher-order questions and problems. And in the digital tutoring example, teachers can leverage technology to better meet students where they are, instructing them inside their homes (remotely), for example. However, without transparency and accountability, digital education can also shift costs onto teachers and parents, abusing their lack of authority in policy settings and magnifying the obstacles that teachers face in teaching well in low-income settings.

We know from years of research that teaching is a complex activity requiring the mastery and delivery of content as well as the ability to make quick and appropriate judgment calls. Therefore, more serious scrutiny is needed of the risks involved in digital education potentially disrupting teachers' social and emotional roles in public schools. In the digital school, Justin's teacher could see that he was struggling socially and emotionally, that his home life was deteriorating, that he came to school hungry and traumatized. With the rise in digital education, it is critical that we understand whether and how digital schools, courses, and tutoring are working with and for teachers to support the conditions identified as essential in low-income settings. We also need to remain very open to the possibility that digital education may be fragmenting teachers' roles into splintered pieces rather than focusing and leveraging teacher resources.

What Drives Curriculum, and What Counts as Knowledge?

There is growing energy around the idea that the enormous variation in what students learn between and across schools and districts is problematic. Much of the conversation seems to focus on the issue of alignment: making sure that common standards and common curricula are the basis for common formal, general education in the United States. The issue at the core of these debates is one of balance: how to ensure that students get courses of equal quality, independent of where they live or their socioeconomic status, while taking into account the critical importance of local context and students' individual needs and experiences. Figure I.1 provides a way to visualize this balance while also considering how instruction and data interplay with curriculum. On one end of the curriculum continuum is *centrally developed curriculum* that typically might be standardized, highly structured, and used across all local contexts and students. On the other end is *locally developed curriculum* that might be created or adapted by teachers in response to students and their local contexts. As we have stressed, there are trade-offs all along the continuum.

A focus on curriculum seems obvious until we see the nuances of what affects curriculum in the digital setting. For one, digital curriculum can be much more tightly intertwined with both instruction and assessment, making it harder to see it as its own entity.

In fact, in the case of software-driven, asynchronous instruction, instruction, assessment, and curriculum are all delivered through the software medium. Second, vendors, much like textbook publishers, play a central role in determining the content of curriculum and, ultimately, what counts as knowledge. When a district purchases a digital course, for example, it is also buying that company's conceptualization of what knowledge matters, particularly when alignment of curriculum to the school day is left to discretion of vendor. Third, digital curriculum is atomized into smaller and smaller units, with students receiving a module on reducing fractions or one on proper pronoun usage.

The decisions vendors make around curriculum have direct influence on the nature and quality of instruction. For example, ABL's deliberate actions to involve teachers in generating locally developed curriculum and to align content both externally and internally expanded learning opportunities for students. In the case of Blended Academy, Pyramid's more centralized decisions around curriculum reduced rather than expanded opportunities for low-income students to learn twenty-first-century skills. The unwieldiness of the curriculum—like the big textbook it is supposed to replace—diverted teachers' and students' time away from strengthening other kinds of knowledge, such as higher-order applied math through project-based learning. And in the case of digital tutoring, some vendors' choices of highly structured, centralized curricula limited the ability of instruction to align with that of students' day schools, while other providers allowed tutors more discretion in putting together curriculum on their own, "local" level, which in turn demanded more capacity and resources from the tutors.

CRITICAL QUESTIONS IN AN URGENT DIALOGUE

The premise of this book is that opportunities to realize the potential of digital education emerge when people working upstream and downstream focus their attention on a common, urgent set of questions and try to begin to understand the links between the questions, their actions, and the outcomes—whether these outcomes are problematic, innovative, or exciting. The questions that have framed analysis in this book—questions about data, instruction, and curriculum—are simultaneously global (upstream) and local (downstream). They are important questions about the changing role of outside vendors in public education and the influence of these vendors on the purposes and outcomes of public education. They are also questions that help us better understand the nature of teaching and learning in digital education—what is being taught, how the technology is being integrated or not, and what it means when we say digital education "works" in our classrooms.

Figures I.1, 6.1, 6.2, and 6.3 are tools for stakeholders in digital education, both downstream and upstream, to use in structuring these critical discussions around data, curriculum and instruction in contracting for digital education. Figure I.1 purposely does not dictate a "best" curriculum format or the instructional design most aligned with the best practices. Instead, it is the role of those closest to the instructional point of delivery to figure out where the particular needs of their schools and students fall on this diagram and then pursue digital education formats that match.

In the three cases of digital education, we show how the interaction between what happens upstream and downstream is not predetermined. Certainly, there are powerful commercial and political influences that are driving all types of digital education. But the elements of setting and context also help determine what digital education ends up offering students in low-income settings. Whether and how vendors, policy makers, and educators mobilize and converse around digital education probably matters a lot more than any one policy or fiat aimed at disciplining the market or getting policy into the digital age. The outcomes of such structured dialogues can bring issues of quality of digital instruction into public view and contribute to the redesign of programs that better serve the needs of students from low-income families.

Scrutinizing the role of both government and vendors in contracts for digital education turns on a serious dialogue around teaching and learning in low-income settings. It also ultimately turns on creating a policy agenda supportive of transparency and accountability. This is work we and many other educators and policy makers are wading through now, attempting to distill what we are learning into concrete policy recommendations. Examples of such changes could include:

- Requiring digital education companies to serve all students, in particular students with disabilities and English language learners
- Creating financial incentives through resource sharing that help offset costs for digital education vendors, such as providing transportation for students with disabilities or providing the hardware (e.g., computer accommodations)
- Establishing minimum qualifications for digital tutors and teachers that are aligned with those required of all public school instructors
- Building the capacity of local and state governments to assess instructional quality in digital education (e.g., through observation tools and protocols for assessing vendor quality)
- Introducing system-changing strategies help offset power asymmetries in contracting for digital education. For example, policies could require vendors receiving public funds to allow districts, parents, and teachers regular access to student assessments (not just summative scores) and to evaluate performance based on rigorous *common* assessments of student progress.

These represent some examples of where policy can go, not the totality of policy recommendations based on our own and others' research.[5]

The considerable potential of digital education to meet its promises to public schools turns on informed policy action. Digital education clearly has staying power, given the might and influence of those driving it and the clear financial incentives for those selling it. But, what *are* we getting, and what is its actual value for students and schools with limited financial resources? Around this issue there is enormous uncertainty and minimal action on the part of policy makers and industry leaders. We must carefully examine both quality and access in digital education, as well as the influence of vendors and policy. In the absence of sustained and equal scrutiny, we lose the potential of digital education to push a broader agenda for more equal redistribution of resources in public education. This would be an enormous loss.

APPENDIX

Research Notes on the Digital Education Cases

THIS BOOK IS a case study of vendor influence in digital education contracting in K–12 public schooling, focusing on embedded case studies of three digital education formats: digital courses, digital curriculum, and digital tutoring. By *case study,* we mean rich, descriptive analysis of a problem or issue where the emphasis is on process rather then explanation or outcome. Sharon Merriam has identified three major types of case studies: descriptive, interpretive, and explanatory.[1] The approach we take here is mainly descriptive in that the phenomenon we are studying is undertheorized and underresearched. However, our analysis is also interpretive in that it draws on rich and in-depth examinations of digital education settings to develop conceptual categories that inform both theory and practice.

CHAPTER 3: LONGITUDINAL PARTICIPATORY RESEARCH ON DIGITAL COURSES

Chapter 3 draws on the longitudinal qualitative research of an actual instructor for Accelerated Blended Learning (ABL). As an example of participatory research, a researcher on our team took her own experiences as a blended learning instructor for ABL and compared it in systematic ways with data from many levels and areas within the organization. Participatory research methods are based on the local knowledge of those experiencing the phenomenon studied, which forms the basis of the research.[2] In other words, those working downstream actually organize, conduct, and analyze the work.

Participatory research offers an intimate view of the instructional setting, how the curriculum functions, the role of the instructor, and how data are used and disseminated. We were interested in looking *inside* examples of effective digital education to figure out how high-quality instructor-driven blended instruction can actually work. How does the instructional strategy relate to the curriculum structure? How does building teacher capacity relate to course design? How does the assessment process relate to data use? How do the face-to-face and digital settings interact? As we have argued throughout the book, the digital classroom can be very difficult to access. As an instructor, the researcher gathered levels of data and particular insights that would have been hard to garner from the outside but that are critical to understanding the setting. If we are to learn from the promising places of digital education, we must get inside them.

The data used for this chapter came from the following sources collected over three years:

- Observations of eight digital courses in which the researcher was an "outsider," which included assignments, responses to assignments, and archived discussion forums
- Participation as an instructor in multiple blended courses (both online and face-to-face sessions) with students
- Participation in multiple, day-long professional development workshops for instructors
- Personal interviews with course instructors
- Personal interviews with program director
- Analysis of archived documents such as course syllabi, instructor and program-level aggregate reports, reports from school-level listening sessions, student participation, and survey reports

CHAPTER 4: AN ETHNOGRAPHIC LONGITUDINAL STUDY OF A DIGITAL SCHOOL

The data used in this chapter are drawn from a larger, longitudinal, qualitative case study. The story it tells is bounded in time from 2011 to 2013. A number of graduate students were critical to the work, conducting countless observations and interviews, developing databases to house digital data, and offering insights and interpretations. The intent of the case study was to provide detailed, contextualized information on multiple aspects of Blended Academy (BA), including school environment and structure, professional development, classroom instructional practice, stakeholder interactions, and governance structure. As such, a wide variety of data was collected, including observations, interviews, focus groups, e-mail correspondence, documents, photographs, and artifacts. We also developed a worksheet for identifying the different sources of revenue and contracts needed to support the digital school. Throughout the year, the research team was at the school two to three days per week and conducted multiple observations of each of the following:

- Teachers' classrooms
- Board meetings
- Professional development
- Afterschool weekly staff meetings
- Recruitment events
- Parent meetings

These formal observations were conducted using an observation protocol that focused on direct quotation and paraphrasing of participants' words, detailed description of practices and interactions among participants, and descriptions of researchers' roles. Informal data was also collected through school walk-throughs and frequent conversations with teachers, administrators, and staff, which were noted in an ongoing field log.

The research team conducted two rounds (early September and mid-March) of semi-structured interviews with the four content teachers, the master intervention teacher, and the student services coordinator. Team members conducted single interviews with the school's founder, principal, and counselor. These interviews ranged in length from sixteen minutes to eighty-six minutes. The first-round interview questions focused on the vision for the school model, expectations for the year, instructional philosophy, and the interviewees' prior experiences and background. The second round of interviews included the founder and the principal and focused on instruction in the classroom as enacted, challenges encountered, strategies used to address challenges, and teachers' self-identified roles in the classroom.

The team held a single round of student focus groups near the beginning of the school year. Each focus group consisted of five students. The intent of the focus groups was to collect data on students' early perceptions of the new school and the use of technology, as well as to gain a sense of students' backgrounds prior to coming to BA, including their previous school experiences. The focus groups were also intended to allow students to provide early feedback to the school. All interviews and focus groups were recorded to ensure accuracy.

The research team also collected information in the form of a variety of useful documents. The team was able to keep a cache of group e-mails to and from teachers and administrators and examples of teacher-created documents for use in the classroom and handouts from various professional developments and staff meetings. The researchers also collected school board agendas, minutes, and budget documents as well as the school's development plans and charter proposal. Finally, team members were given access to the digital curriculum, enabling a close examination of the content curriculum to accompany the observational data of its use in the classroom. The researchers entered all transcripts, observational field notes, and memos into NVivo qualitative analysis software. The collected data include interview transcripts, observational field notes, e-mails, and archival documents.

CHAPTER 5: AN INTEGRATED, LONGITUDINAL, MIXED-METHOD CASE STUDY OF DIGITAL TUTORING

The longitudinal, mixed-method study that informed chapter 5 integrated quasi-experimental analysis of impacts on student achievement with an in-depth, qualitative examination of the intervention in practice. From 2006 to 2009 our study worked in one large urban district and from 2009 to 2013 in collaboration with six large urban school districts ranging in size from 85,000 to 650,000 students. Our research team spanned three universities: University of Southern California, University of Texas–Austin, and University of Wisconsin–Madison. Our analytic process was part of our fully integrated mixed-method research design, where the quantitative and qualitative teams coordinated and collaborated at all stages of the study (design, collection, analysis, and dissemination). Specifically, the qualitative and quantitative teams met to review analytical findings from both study components, direct additional data collection, refine analysis plans, and prepare dissemination of findings to stakeholders.

For the purposes of analysis, a *digital* provider is one that uses a digital platform (software or live tutor via a technological platform such as a computer, netbook, or hand-held device) as an intentional, integral, and consistent part of its instructional strategy in delivering supplemental education services (SES) to eligible students in at least one of the five districts in our study. Students served by these providers consistently used digital instructional tools for at least half of their tutoring experience. Our qualitative sample of five digital providers represents each of the subcategories of digital providers, including synchronous, asynchronous, all digital, and blended.

Categorization of digital providers outside of our qualitative sample proved difficult for a number of reasons. First, it is difficult to find a single, consistent source of program descriptions. On a number of occasions the program description in providers' state applications differed from the description in district parent information. Second, some providers were described as having digital platforms one year but not the next. Third, there are many different types of digital platforms. Other studies of digital learning have faced similar challenges in categorizing providers, but few have attempted rigorous identification of subcategories.

The qualitative research focused on provider instructional practice in different program models and settings, the nature and quality of tutoring provided, and district-level program administration across multiple districts. Our examination was grounded in two key principles: a sustained focus on instructional setting and a sharp focus on the system of out-of-school-time (OST) implementers—classroom teachers, providers, parents, tutors, school personnel, district, and state staff—who enabled or impeded the effectiveness of OST tutoring interventions. This data included:

- Observations of full tutoring sessions using a classroom observation instrument designed to capture key features of both digital and nondigital instructional settings
- Interviews with provider administrators about the structure of instructional programs, choice of curricula and assessments, challenges in implementation, and choices in staffing
- Interviews with tutoring staff about instructional formats, curriculum, adaptations for special student needs, staff professional background, and training
- Interviews with district and state administrators involved in program implementation
- Parent focus groups with parents of students who were eligible to receive SES, most with children currently receiving SES
- Document analysis of formal curriculum materials from providers; diagnostic, formative, or final assessments used; and policy documents on federal, state, or district policies concerning the implementation of SES.

A centerpiece of our qualitative work is a standardized observation instrument for use in both nondigital and digital tutoring settings. Because these settings can be quite different, this instrument includes indicators to specifically respond to digital settings without a live tutor (e.g., instructional software that adapts to students' instructional needs) as well as to better describe how technology is used to improve instruction (e.g., use technology to employ higher-order thinking skills) and address issues around access (e.g., technology is reliable and accessible to all students).

The sample frame for our quantitative data included eligible students, registered students, and those attending supplemental services in the six districts in our study. We drew on elementary, middle, and high school data from the administration of standardized tests and administrative databases for managing supplemental services programs, as well as student transcript and demographic data from the districts. These data were used in constructing measures of receipt of supplemental services, student-level controls to account for selection into supplemental services, and the outcome measures (i.e., changes in tests scores). In estimating the impacts of supplemental services on student achievement, our quantitative team used an interrupted time series design with internal comparison groups and multiple non-experimental approaches (value-added, student fixed effects, school and student fixed effects, and propensity score-matching models) to control for school and student time invariant characteristics. The level of access to these digital courses, schools and tutoring, and subsequent data collection processes would not have been possible without the help of educators and administrative staff at ABL, BA, and the sample districts in the case of OST tutoring.

NOTES

CHAPTER 1

1. Arne Duncan, "Choosing the Right Battle: Remarks and a Conversation" (remarks presented at the American Education Research Association, San Francisco, April 2013).

2. Barack Obama, "Preparing a 21st Century Workforce: Science, Technology, Engineering, and Mathematics (STEM) Education in the 2014 Budget," White House, http://www.whitehouse.gov/sites/default/files/microsites/ostp/2014_R&Dbudget_STEM.pdf.

3. For history on early federal investments in virtual schools, see Andrew Zucker and Robert Kozma, *The Virtual High School: Teaching Generation V* (New York: Teachers College Press, 2003). Michael Barbour also writes about these schools in "The Landscape of K–12 Online Learning," in *Handbook of Distance Learning*, 3rd ed., ed. Michael Grahame Moore (New York: Routledge, 2013), 574–590.

4. See www.inbloom.org.

5. Michelle Molnar, "Researchers Estimate 7,600 District Buyers for Common Core Materials K–12," *Education Week*, November 27, 2013, blogs.edweek.org/edweek/marketplacek12/2013/11/researchers_estimate_7600_district_buyers_for_common_core_materials.html.

6. Kevin Carey, "Education Funding and Low-Income Children: A Review of Current Research," Center on Budget and Policy Priorities, November 2002, http://www.cbpp.org/cms.

7. Nicholas Johnson, Phil Oliff, and Jeremy Koulish, "Most States Are Cutting Education," Center on Budget and Policy Priorities, February 2009, http://www.cbpp.org/cms.

8. Carey, "Education Funding and Low-Income Children."

9. See, for example, D. W. Shaffer, K. Squire, R. Halverson, and J. P. Gee, "Video Games and the Future of Learning," *Phi Delta Kappan* 67, no. 5 (2005): 105–111.

10. For a discussion of learning practices linked to low-income students' higher performance on achievement tests, see Trish Williams, Michael Kirst, and Edward Haertel, "Similar Students, Different Results: Why Do Some Schools Do Better?" 2005, www.edsource.org.

11. Ibid.

12. Linda Darling-Hammond and John Bransford, eds., *Preparing Teachers for a Changing World: What Teachers Should Learn and Be Able to Do* (San Francisco: Wiley, 2007).

13. Mizuko Ito et al., *Connected Learning: An Agenda for Research and Design* (Irvine, CA: Digital Media and Learning Research Hub, 2013).

14. Shaffer, Squire, Halverson, and Gee, "Video Games and the Future of Learning."

15. Regina Figueiredo-Brown, discussion with the authors, July 16, 2013.

16. James Gee, discussion with the authors, June 10, 2013.

17. Regina Figueiredo-Brown, "How Online Schools Serve and Fail to Serve At-Risk Students" (PhD diss., University of Wisconsin–Madison, 2013).

18. Jeannie Oakes, *Keeping Track: How Schools Structure Inequality* (New Haven, CT: Yale University Press, 2005).

19. Greg J. Duncan and Jeanne Brooks-Gunn, eds., *Consequences of Growing Up Poor* (New York: Russell Sage Foundation, 1997).

20. Susan Aud et al., *The Condition of Education 2012*, NCES 2012-045 (Washington, DC: National Center for Education Statistics, 2012).

21. Diane Ravitch, "This Is Your Homework: Berliner on Education and Inequality," *A Site to Discuss Better Education for All,* July 23, 2012, http://dianeravitch.net/.

22. The importance of looking simultaneously at macro and micro dynamics in education policy is central to the work of Stephen Ball; see, for example, *Education Policy and Social Class: The Selected Works of Stephen J. Ball* (New York: Routledge World Library of Educationalists, 2005).

23. "Private Ventures for the Public Good: A Campaign to Change Conversation, Opinions and Opportunities," Education Industry Association, http://www.educationindustry.org/education-industry-foundation-2 2012.

24. Ibid.

25. Katie Ash,"Blended Learning Models Generating Lessons Learned," *Education Week* 31, no. 19 (2012): 10.

26. Ellis Booker, "Education Tech Investments Surpassed $1 Billion in 2012," *Information Week Education,* January 25, 2013, www.informationweek.com/education/online-learning.

27. "K12 Inc. purchased K–12 Assets from Kaplan Virtual Education," *Manda-Soft: The DNA of Mergers & Acquisitions,* May 19, 2011, http://mandasoft.com/segmentview.aspx.

28. Matthew Panzarino, "Apple Partners with DK, Pearson, McGraw Hill and Houghton Mifflin Harcourt for Textbooks," *The Next Web,* January 9, 2012.

29. Tom Vander Ark, "Smart Cities: New York City Is an EdTech Hotspot," *Education Week,* November 26, 2012.

30. Christopher Nyren, "Educelerate: Chicago's Central Role in EdTech Innovation," *EdReach,* November 29, 2012, http://edreach.us/2012/11/29/educelerate-chicagos-central-role-in-edtech-innovation/.

31. As reported in *District Administration: Solutions for School District Management Media Kit*, 2013, http://www.districtadministration.com/media.

32. Barbara Queen, Laurie Lewis, and Jared Coopersmith, *Distance Education Courses for Public Elementary and Secondary School Students: 2009–2010* (Washington, DC: U.S. Department of Education, 2011).

33. Cassandra Rowand, *Teacher Use of Computers and the Internet in Public Schools* (Washington, DC: National Center for Education Statistics, 2000).

34. Lucinda Gray, Nina Thomas, and Laurie Lewis, *Teachers' Use of Educational Technology in U.S. Public Schools: 2009* (Washington, DC: National Center for Education Statistics, 2010).

35. The reported findings are from a survey conducted by The Pew Internet and American Life Project. The survey was conducted online and included a non-probability sample of 2,462 (mainly public) middle and high school teachers. One in-person and two online focus groups were also conducted to support the findings from the survey. The sample is skewed toward teachers teaching mainly academically successful students. See "The Pew Internet and American Life Project," http://www.pewinternet.org/.

36. "Fast Facts about Online Learning," iNACOL, http://www.inacol.org/cms/wp-content/uploads/2013/04/iNACOL_FastFacts_Feb2013.pdf.

37. I. Elaine Allen and Jeff Seaman, *Going the Distance: Online Education in the United States, 2011* (Newburyport, MA: Sloan Consortium, 2011).

38. John Watson, Amy Murin, Lauren Vashaw, Butch Gemin, and Chris Rapp, *Keeping Pace with K–12 Online Learning: An Annual Review of Policy and Practice, 2011* (Durango, CO: Evergreen Education Group, 2011).

39. Ron Packard, "Interview with the CEO and Founder: K12 Inc.," *Wall Street Transcript*, September 7, 2011.

40. Kelsey Sheehy, "States, Districts Require Online Ed for High School Graduation," *US News & World Report*, October 24, 2012; Michelle Davis, "States, Districts Move to Require Virtual Classes," *Education Week*, October 17, 2011.

41. Gary Stager, "The Possibilities of Online Learning," *New York Times*, April 6, 2011.

42. National Association of Colleges and Employers, *FERPA Primer: The Basics and Beyond*, 2012, www.naceweb.org/public/ferpa.

43. "Google Apps for Education," http://www.google.com/enterprise/apps/education/.

44. Rebecca Shulman, "The King of Mooc Abdicates the Throne," *Slate*, November 19, 2013, www.slate.com/articles/life/education/2013/11/sebastian_thrun_and_udacity_distance_learning_is_unsuccessful_for_most_students.html.

45. Katrina E. Bulkley and Patricia Burch, "The Changing Nature of Private Engagement in Public Education: For-Profit and Nonprofit Organizations and Educational Reform," *Peabody Journal of Education* 86, no. 3 (2011): 236–251.

46. Patricia Burch, *Hidden Markets: The New Education Privatization* (New York: Routledge, 2009).

47. "Overview of the Education Industry Association," 2010, http://www .educationindustry.org/tier.asp?sid=1.

48. Martha Minow, "Public and Private Partnerships: Accounting for the New Religion," *Harvard Law Review* 116 (2002): 1230; Harvey B. Feigenbaum and Jeffrey R. Henig, "The Political Underpinnings of Privatization," *World Politics* 46, no. 2 (1994): 185.

49. Bulkley and Burch, "The Changing Nature of Private Engagement," 236–251.

50. Catherine DiMartino, "Bringing Transparency to New "Hybrid" Schools: Introducing a Continuum of Control" (paper presented at the American Education Research Assocation, Denver, May 2010), 5.

51. An example of President Obama being influenced by the banking industry is his decision to not support a law that would have allowed bankruptcy judges to modify onerous mortgages.

52. Amir Hefetz and Mildred Warner, "Privatization and Its Reverse: Explaining the Dynamics of the Government Contracting Process," *Journal of Public Administration Research and Theory* 14, no. 2 (2004): 171–190; H. George Frederickson, "Public Ethics and the New Managerialism: An Axiomatic Theory," in *Ethics in Public Management*, ed. H. George Frederickson and Richard K. Ghere (Armonk, NY: M. E. Sharpe, 2005), 165–183.

53. Carolyn J. Heinrich, "Third-Party Governance Under No Child Left Behind: Accountability and Performance Management Challenges," *Journal of Public Administration Research and Theory* 20, supp. no. 1 (2010): i59–i80.

54. On these points, see for example, Clive R. Belfield, "The Evidence on Education Vouchers: An Application to the Cleveland Scholarship and Tutoring Program" (draft of a paper prepared for the Conference on Education and Economic Development, Cleveland, OH, November 2005), 17–18; Natalie Lacireno-Paquet, Thomas T. Holyoke, Michele Moser, and Jeffrey R. Henig, "Creaming versus Cropping: Charter School Enrollment Practices in Response to Market Incentives," *Educational Evaluation and Policy Analysis* 24, no. 2 (2002): 145–158. For an excellent discussion of this literature, please also see Molly Stewart, "Design and Implementation of an Equity-Oriented Choice Program" (PhD diss., University of Wisconsin–Madison, 2013).

CHAPTER 2

1. There will always be individual cases that exceed or fall below expectations.

2. Thanks to Donna Lewis for bringing our attention to this example.

3. Edward Wyatt, "F.C.C. Backs Plan to Update a Fund That Helps Connect Schools to the Internet," *New York Times*, July 19, 2013.

4. "Education First," http://www.education-first.com/.

5. Arne Duncan, "The New Platform for Learning," U.S. Department of Education, March 2012, http://www.ed.gov/news/speeches/new-platform-learning.

6. Neal Riley, "Arne Duncan Promotes Digital Education," *San Francisco Chronicle*, September 8, 2012.

7. Wyatt, "F.C.C. Backs Plan."

8. Clayton Christensen, Curtis W. Johnson, and Michael B. Horn, *Disrupting Class: How Disruptive Innovation Will Change the Way the World Learns* (New York: McGraw-Hill, 2008); M. B. Horn, "Disrupting Class and the Future of Learning" (guest lecture, University of Southern California, Los Angeles, October 2012).

9. Clayton M. Christensen, Michael B. Horn, and Heather Staker, *Is K–12 Blended Learning Disruptive? An Introduction of the Theory of Hybrids* (San Francisco: Clayton Christensen Institute, 2013).

10. "About Startl," http://startl.org/about/.

11. "KnowledgeWorks and New Technology Foundations Join Forces to Transform Approach to High School Education in the U.S.," *Business Wire*, March 9, 2009, http://www.businesswire.com/news/home/20090309006211/en/Knowledge Works-Technology-Foundations-Join-Forces-Transform-Approach.

12. On Jeb Bush and digital education, also see J. Van Galen, "Learning in the Digital Age: Control or Connection," *Rethinking Schools* 27, no. 2 (2012), http://www.rethinkingschools.org/restrict.asp?path=archive/27_02/27_02_vangalen.shtml.

13. Jeb Bush, "Students Should Have the Choice of Digital Schools," *CNN*, January 31, 2013, http://schoolsofthought.blogs.cnn.com/2013/01/.

14. Denis Newman, "Conducting and Reporting Product Evaluation Research," Software and Information Industry Association, November 2011, www.siaa.net.

15. Gregory Ferenstein, "How Bill Gates's Favorite Teacher Wants to Disrupt Education," *Fast Company*, February 17, 2011.

16. Heather Staker, "The Rise of K-12 Blended Learning: Profiles of Emerging Models," Innosight Institute, May 2011, http://www.innosightinstitute.org/innosight/wp-content/uploads/2011/05/The-Rise-of-K-12-Blended-Learning.pdf.

17. "Catapult.org Launches First Crowdfunding Site Focused on Equality for Girls and Women," *Women Deliver*, October 11, 2012, http://www.women deliver.org/updates/entry/catapult.org-launches-first-crowdfunding-site-focused-on-equality-for-girls.

18. Jonathan R. Macey, *Corporate Governance: Promises, Kept, Promises Broken* (Princeton, NJ: Princeton University Press, 2008).

19. A century-long research base examines the relationship between media and education. As Richard Clark argued in his well-cited 1983 meta-analyses, studies of the influence of media on learning have been a fixed feature of educational research since Cecil Thorndike recommended pictures as a labor saving device in instruction in 1912. Most of this research is buttressed by the hope

that learning will be enhanced with the proper mix of medium, student, subject matter, content, and learning task. A typical study compares the relative achievement of groups that have received similar subject matter from different media. See Richard Clark, "Reconsidering Research on Learning from Media," *Review of Educational Research* 53, no. 4 (1983): 445–459.

20. Ibid.

21. Ibid.

22. Ibid. As one of these competing explanations, Clark identifies the tendency of studies to confound effects on learning with other kinds of indirect effects, such as cost of learning. He also argues that studies showing effects are biased by editorial decisions favoring studies that have large effects and use newer media.

23. Robert Kozma, "Learning with Media," *Review of Educational Research* 61, no. 2 (1991): 179–211.

24. Ibid.

25. Ibid.

26. George Lucas Educational Foundation, *Edutopia: Success Stories for Learning in the Digital Age* (San Francisco: Jossey-Bass, 2002).

27. Larry Cuban, *Teachers and Machines: The Classroom Use of Technology since 1920* (New York: Teachers College Press, 1986); Larry Cuban, *Oversold and Underused: Computers in the Classroom* (Cambridge, MA: Harvard University Press, 2001); Allan Collins and Richard Halverson, *Rethinking Education in the Age of Technology: The Digital Revolution and Schooling in America* (New York: Teachers College Press, 2009).

28. James Gee, *Good Video Games and Good Learning: Collected Essays on Video Games, Learning and Literacy* (New York: Peter Lang, 2007); Collins and Halverson, *Rethinking Education in the Age of Technology*; Cuban, *Oversold and Underused*; Larry Cuban, "Computers versus Classrooms: Classrooms Win," *Teachers College Record* 95, no. 2 (1993): 185–210.

29. Robert Bernard et al., "How Does Distance Education Compare with Classroom Instruction? A Meta-Analysis of the Empirical Literature," *Review of Educational Research* 74, no. 3 (2004): 379–439.

30. Ibid.

31. Heather Staker and Michael Horn, *Classifying K–12 Blended Learning*, Innosight Institute, May 2012, www.innosightinstitute.org.

32. Russell Osguthorpe and Charles Graham, "Blended Learning Environments: Definitions and Directions," *Quarterly Review of Distance Education* 4, no. 3 (2003): 227–233. The literature in this chapter is applicable to more than one of the cases, whereas specific literature (e.g., on out-of-school time) is located in the relevant chapter. Blended learning effectiveness literature is relevant to online schools and curated curriculum and therefore is included here.

33. In order to gain a comprehensive understanding of the previous research in the area of blended learning, we searched several iterations of *blended learning*,

including *hybrid school, hybrid learning, online leaning, distance education, virtual education,* and *virtual school,* both alone and in conjunction with *K–12 education* or *compulsory education.* Additionally, we explored the publications of several policy centers and private research institutes, such as the Education Development Center, National Education Policy Center, and Innosight Institute. We carefully reviewed all relevant research and categorized it as policy context, blended learning definitions, and/or hybrid school evaluation or implementation.

34. John Watson, *Blending Learning: The Convergence of Online and Face-to-Face Education,* North American Council for Online Learning, 2008, http://www .inacol.org/resources/publications/inacol-report/; Daniel Light, Tim Reitzes, and Michelle Cerrone, "Evaluation of the School of One Summer Pilot: An Experiment in Individualized Instruction," Center for Children and Technology Education Development Center, October 2009, http://schoolofone.org/resources/ edc_2009_eval.pdf; Barbara Queen, Laurie Lewis, and Jared Coopersmith, *Distance Education Courses for Public Elementary and Secondary School Students: 2009–2010* (Washington, DC: U.S. Department of Education, 2011).

35. Cathy Cavanaugh, Kathy Jo Gillan, Jeff Kromrey, Melinda Hess and Robert Blomeyer, *The Effects of Distance Education on K–12 Student Outcomes: A Meta-Analysis* (Naperville, IL: North Central Regional Educational Laboratory, October 2004); Rachel Cole, James J. Kemple, and Micha D. Segeritz. *Assessing the Early Impact of School of One: Evidence from Three School-Wide Pilots,* Research Alliance for New York City Schools, 2012, http://steinhardt. nyu.edu/research_alliance/publications/So1_June2012#.Up1bOY1Q0QI; Jonathan Margolin, Briana Kleidon, Ryan Williams, and Michele Cranwell Schmidt, *Vermont's Title II-D: Enhancing Education Through Technology Program,* American Institutes for Research, November 2011, http://www.air.org/files/Vermont_ Ed-Tech_Report_FINAL_2011.pdf.

36. Barbara Means, Yukie Toyama, Robert Murphy, Marianne Bakia and Karla Jones, *Evaluation of Evidence-Based Practices in Online Learning: A Meta-Analysis and Review of Online Learning Studies,* U.S. Department of Education, September 2010, http://www2.ed.gov/rschstat/eval/tech/evidence-based-practices/finalreport.pdf. Also see Barbara Means, Yukie Toyama, Robert Murphy and Marianne Bakia, "The Effectiveness of Online and Blended Learning: A Meta-Analysis of the Empirical Literature," *Teachers College Record,* 115, no. 3 (2013): 1–47.

37. Means et al., "Evaluation of Evidence-Based Practices in Online Learning."

38. Ibid.

39. Light, Reitzes, and Cerrone, "Evaluation of the School of One Summer Pilot."

40. Ibid., 2.

41. Cole, Kemple, and Segeritz, "Assessing the Early Impact of School of One."

42. Means et al., "Evaluation of Evidence-Based Practices"; Yong Zhao, Jing Lei, Bo Yan, Chun Lai, and Sophia Tan, "What Makes the Difference? A Practical

Analysis of Research on the Effectiveness of Distance Education," *Teachers College Record* 107, no. 8 (2005): 1836–1884.

43. I. Elaine Allen and Jeff Seaman, *Changing Course: Ten Years of Tracking Online Education in the United States,* Babson Survey Research Group, 2013, http://files.eric.ed.gov/fulltext/ED541571.pdf; Curtis Bonk and Charles Graham, eds., *The Handbook of Blended Learning: Global Perspectives, Local Designs* (San Francisco: John Wiley & Sons, 2006); Means et al., "Evaluation of Evidence-Based Practices"; Zhao et al., "What Makes the Difference?"

44. See Mark Warschauer and Tina Matuchniak, "New Technology and Digital Worlds: Analyzing Evidence of Equity and Access, Use, and Outcomes," *Review of Research in Education* 34, no. 1 (2010), 179–225; S. Craig Watkins, "Digital Divide: Navigating the Digital Edge," *International Journal of Learning and Media* 3 no. 2 (2011): 1–12.

45. Staker, "The Rise of K-12 Blended Learning"; Gary Miron and Jessica Urschel, *Understanding and Improving Full Time Virtual Schools* (Boulder, CO: National Education Policy Center, 2012); Linda Shear, Yukie Toyama, and Austin Lasseter, *Understanding the Implications of Online Learning for Educational Productivity,* U.S. Department of Education, Office of Educational Technology, 2012, http://www.sri.com/sites/default/files/publications/implications-online-learning.pdf.

46. Paul Goldenberg, *Thinking (and Talking) About Technology in Math Classrooms* (Newton, MA: Education Development Center, 2000).

47. Robert Yagelski and Sarah Powley, "Virtual Connections and Real Boundaries: Teaching Writing and Preparing Writing Teachers on the Internet," *Computers and Composition* 13, no. 1 (1996): 25–36.

48. Chen-Lin Kulik and James Kulik, "Effectiveness of Computer-Based Instruction: An Updated Analysis," *Computers in Human Behavior* 7 (1991): 75–99; Mark Warschauer, *Laptops and Literacy: Learning in the Wireless Classroom* (New York; Teachers College Press, 2006).

49. As noted by William Tierney, "Beyond the Ivory Tower: The Role of the Intellectual in Eliminating Poverty" (presidential address,annual meeting of the American Educational Research Association, San Francisco, April 2013).

50. Kathryn Zickuhr and Aaron Smith, *Digital Differences,* Pew Research Center, April 2012, http://pewinternet.org/~/media/Files/Reports/2012/PIP_Digital_differences_041312.pdf.

51. Ibid.

52. Ibid., 56.

53. Ibid., 42.

54. A study conducted by the U.S. Department of Education shows that there is slightly more enrollment in distance education for districts with a poverty concentration of 20 percent or more (84 percent) than in districts with less than 10 percent poverty concentration (81 percent)., Queen et al., *Distance Education Courses.*

55. Miron and Urschel, "Understanding and Improving Full-Time Virtual Schools."

56. John Watson, Amy Murin, Lauren Vashaw, Butch Gemin, and Chris Rapp, *Keeping Pace with K–12 Online Learning: An Annual Review of Policy and Practice*, Evergreen Education Group, 2011, http://kpk12.com.

57. Zickuhr and Smith, "Digital Differences."

58. Michael Barbour, Regina Brown, Lisa Hasler-Waters, Rebecca Hoey, et al., *Online and Blended Learning: A Survey of Policy and Practice from K–12 Schools Around the World*, (Vienna, VA: iNACOL, 2011).

59. *Zero to Eight: Children's Media Use in America*, Common Sense Media, 2011, http://www.commonsensemedia.org/research/zero-eight-childrens-media-use-america.

CHAPTER 3

1. Accelerated Blended Learning is a pseudonym, as are all names of people, vendors, and districts throughout this book.

2. See the appendix for a more detailed description of the research design.

3. "Enrollment by Student Group," Department of Public Instruction; full citation omitted to protect anonymity of case. Also, the current data collection system for ABL has not been able to accurately collect student demographic data on race and ethnicity. Students fill this information out in a pre-course survey, and the current system has errors that omitted up to a third of the students' descriptions of their racial and ethnic backgrounds. Therefore, we did not use this data.

4. Laurence J. O'Toole and Kenneth J. Meier, "Parkinson's Law and the New Public Management? Contracting Determinants and Service—Quality Consequences in Public Education," *Public Administration Review* 64, no. 3 (2004): 342–352.

5. Sue Shellenbarger, "For AP Students a New Classroom Is Online," *Wall Street Journal*, April 20, 2011, http://online.wsj.com/article/SB10001424052748703 922504576272872529316328.html. Chapter 2 discusses much of the context behind blended learning contracting.

6. Andrew Porter, "Curriculum Assessment," in *Handbook of Complementary Methods in Education Research*, ed. Judith L. Green, Gregory Camilli, Patricia B. Elmore, and Elizabeth Grace (Mahwah, NJ: Lawrence Erlbaum, 2006), 141–159.

7. Susan M. Drake and Rebecca Crawford Burns, *Meeting Standards Through Integrated Curriculum* (Alexandria, VA: ASCD, 2004).

8. Barbara Queen and Laurie Lewis, *Distance Education Courses for Public Elementary and Secondary School Students: 2009–10. First Look,* NCES 2012-008 (Washington, DC: National Center for Education Statistics, 2011).

9. Bloom's Digital Taxonomy offers a useful frame identifying the behaviors and actions that are an essential component of learning, especially in the pursuit of higher-order thinking. See Andrew Churches, "Bloom's Digital

Taxonomy," Educational Origami, http://edorigami.wikispaces.com/Bloom's Digital Taxonomy.

10. The individual teacher reports are one-page summaries of various data points collected through the online platform and online surveys of students, parents, and school-level coordinators. It includes specific, instructor-level data on the number and types of learning goals assigned; modes of alignment; student growth as a reader, writer, and thinker and in interaction; number of forum posts; and ratings given to student assignments. The aggregate reports sent out to stakeholders outside of the organization (school- and district-level staff, parents, and funders) include information on areas such as enrollment trends and demographics, student satisfaction ratings, tuition and funding, narrative excerpts on feedback, teacher professional development, and the number of courses offered.

CHAPTER 4

1. All names of places and people are pseudonyms.
2. Christensen, Horn, and Staker, *Is K-12 Blended Learning Disruptive?*
3. The school came under new leadership in 2013.
4. We expected the school to work on this problem in the future so that the withdrawal data, in the words of the programmer, "yielded more value."

CHAPTER 5

1. See the appendix for additional detail on the research design.
2. For example, Linda Price, John Richardson, and Anne Jelfs, "Face-to-Face versus Online Tutoring Support in Distance Education," *Studies in Higher Education* 32, no.1 (2007): 1–20; Cheryl Slattery, *The Impact of a Computer-Based Training System on Strengthening Phonemic Awareness and Increasing Reading Ability Level* (PhD diss., Widener University, 2003); Rebecca A. London, Manuel Pastor Jr., and Rachel Rosner, "When the Divide Isn't Just Digital: How Technology-Enriched Afterschool Programs Help Immigrant Youth Find a Voice, a Place and a Future," *Afterschool Matters*, Spring 2008, http://www.niost.org/pdf/afterschoolmatters/asm_2008_7_spring/asm_2008_7_spring-1.pdf.
3. The literature base on quality tutoring is substantial, offering insight into elements of quality tutoring programs, whether digital or not. Tutoring programs should contain content-rich, differentiated curriculum that is connected to students' school day. Effective instruction is best organized into small grouping patterns, as well as consistent, sustained, varied, active, focused, sequenced, and explicit. Programs should hire and retain tutors with both content and pedagogical knowledge and provide instructional staff with continuous support and authentic evaluation. Programs should actively support positive relationships at

the classroom level among tutors and students, as well as between programs and the surrounding community. Megan Beckett, Geoffrey Borman, Jeffrey Capizzano, Danette Parsley, et al., *Structuring Out-of-School Time to Improve Academic Achievement. IES Practice Guide*, NCES 2009-012 (Washington, DC: Institute of Education Sciences, 2009); George Farkas and Rachel E. Durham, "The Role of Tutoring in Standards-Based Reform," in *Standards-Based Reform and the Poverty Gap: Lessons for No Child Left Behind*, ed. Adam Gamoran (Washington, DC: Brookings Institution, 2007), 201–228; Patricia A. Lauer, Motoko Akiba, Stephanie B. Wilkerson, Helen S. Apthorp, et al., "Out-of-School-Time Programs: A Meta-Analysis of Effects for At-Risk Students," *Review of Educational Research* 76, no. 2 (2006): 275–313; Priscilla Little, Christopher Wimer, and Heather B. Weiss, "After School Programs in the 21st Century: Their Potential and What It Takes to Achieve It," *Issues and Opportunities in Out-of-School Time Evaluation* 10, nos. 1–12 (2008); Joseph A. Durlak and Roger P. Weissberg, "The Impact of After-School Programs That Promote Personal and Social Skills," CASEL, 2007, http://www.casel.org; Deborah Vandell, Elizabeth R. Reisner, and Kim M. Pierce, *Outcomes Linked to High-Quality Afterschool Programs: Longitudinal Findings from the Study of Promising Afterschool Programs*, Policy Studies Associates, 2007, http://files.eric.ed.gov/fulltext/ED499113.pdf.

4. When SES programs are oversubscribed, many districts narrow eligibility requirements to subgroups based on criteria such as grade level, disability status, or proficiency levels on standardized tests. Depending on the school identified as in need of improvement, SES-eligible students can range in grade level from kindergarten to twelfth grade. Our own quantitative analysis suggests a number of trends in attendance rates by student group. Students are more likely to attend if they registered for and attended SES in the prior school year (47–146 percent greater odds), are elementary-level students (25–70 percent higher odds), and are eligible for free lunch (often a criteria for eligibility). Students are less likely to attend SES if they are more frequently absent from regular school (72–99 percent and 7–12 percent lower odds, respectively) and are students with disabilities (15–21 percent lower odds), unless prioritized for eligibility. There are no particular eligibility requirements for students to enroll in digital providers, although some providers (both digital and nondigital) do not offer services for English language learners or students with disabilities.

5. Melissa K. Barnhart, "The Impact of Participation in Supplemental Educational Services (SES) on Student Achievement: 2009–10," Los Angeles Unified School District, Program Evaluation and Research Branch, 2011, http://www.edsource.org/today/wp-content/uploads/Impact-of-SES-2009-10.pdf; Burch, *Hidden Markets*; John Deke, Lisa Dragoset, Karen Bogen, and Brian Gill, "Impacts of Title I Supplemental Educational Services on Student Achievement," NCEE 2012-4053, Institute of Education Sciences, 2012, http://ies.ed.gov/ncee/pubs/20124053/pdf/20124053.pdf; Carolyn J. Heinrich, Robert H. Meyer, and Greg Whitten,

"Supplemental Education Services Under No Child Left Behind Who Signs Up, and What Do They Gain?" *Educational Evaluation and Policy Analysis* 32, no. 2 (2010): 273–298; David Heistad, "Evaluation of Supplemental Education Services in Minneapolis Public Schools: An Application of Matched Sample Statistical Design," Minneapolis Public Schools, 2007, http://rea.mpls.k12 .mn.us/uploads/2004-05_year_1_and_2005-2006_year_2_mps_supplemental _educational_services_evaluation_report.pdf; Carolyn J. Hill, Howard S. Bloom, Alison Rebeck Black, and Mark W. Lipsey, "Empirical Benchmarks for Interpreting Effect Sizes in Research," *Child Development Perspectives* 2, no. 3 (2008): 172–177; Matthew G. Springer, "Supplemental Educational Services and Student Test Score Gains: Evidence from a Large, Urban School District" (working paper, Vanderbilt University, 2009); Ron Zimmer, Brian Gill, Kevin Booker, and J. R. Lockwood III, *State and Local Implementation of the No Child Left Behind Act: Volume I—Title I School Choice, Supplemental Educational Services, and Student Achievement: A Report from the National Longitudinal Study of No Child Left Behind,* U.S. Department of Education, 2007, http://www2.ed.gov/rschstat/eval/choice/implementation/achievementanalysis. pdf; Ron Zimmer, Laura Hamilton, and Rachel Christina, "After-School Tutoring in the Context of No Child Left Behind: Effectiveness of Two Programs in the Pittsburgh Public Schools," *Economics of Education Review* 29, no. 1 (2010): 18–28; Carolyn J. Heinrich and Hiren Nisar, "The Efficacy of Private Sector Providers in Improving Public Educational Outcomes," *American Educational Research Journal* 50, no. 5 (2013): 856–894.

6. Heinrich et al., "Supplemental Education Services under No Child Left Behind"; Heinrich and Nisar, "The Efficacy of Private Sector"; Lauer et al., "Out-of-School-Time Programs."

7. Annalee Good, Patricia Burch, Carolyn Heinrich, Molly Stewart, and Rudy Acosta, "Instruction Matters: Lessons from a Mixed-Method Evaluation of Out of School Time Tutoring under No Child Left Behind," *Teachers College Record* 116, no. 3 (in press).

8. If the district itself is not identified as in need of improvement, it can become one of the many tutoring providers but is subject to the same application requirements at the state level and to contracting at the district level. None of the digital providers discussed in this chapter is a district provider.

9. *The No Child Left Behind Act of 2001,* Title I, Section 1116(e)(3)(A-C), http:// www2.ed.gov/policy/elsec/leg/esea02/pg2.html#sec1116.

10. Maia Cucchiara, Eva Gold, and Elaine Simon, "Contracts, Choice, and Customer Service: Marketization and Public Engagement in Education," *Teachers College Record* 113, no. 11 (2011): 2460–2502; Martha Minow, "Public and Private Partnerships: Accounting for the New Religion," *Harvard Law Review,* 116 (2002): 1229.

11. Stewart, *Design and Implementation.*

12. In addition to tutors, a number of providers had staff farther from the point of instructional delivery who interact with a student's instructional process. This includes case managers, teacher leaders/monitors, curriculum managers, counselors or case managers who contact parents and the school district if there are issues or questions about students' progress, and prescription monitors, who periodically review student files, adjust the sequence or pace of the learning program, and continually train tutors. There are also provider staff involved in instructional delivery who do not interact with students or their files. For example, there are curriculum teams that continue to develop and revise the curriculum and quality assurance testers who test the curriculum once it is inserted into the software platform.

13. A third option is using open-source software, such as Moodle or Sakai, which is free and allows users to adapt and develop them for their own purposes. None of the providers in this study uses open-source software for instructional platforms.

14. And although the technology allows for a lot of interaction between tutor and student, technical challenges are common and interrupt instruction.

15. There have been a number of high-profile investigations of SES vendors for fraudulent practices around invoicing, including a federal lawsuit filed in 2012 against the *Princeton Review*. See Jennifer Preston, "Princeton Review Accused of Fraud in Tutoring Services," *New York Times*, May 1, 2012, http://www.nytimes.com/2012/05/02/nyregion/princeton-review-accused-of-fraud-in-tutoring-program.html?_r=0; Kristyn Hartman and Joel Chow, "State Investigates Tutor Service: Organization no Longer Used by Columbus City Schools," *Columbus Dispatch*, July 26, 2012, http://www.dispatch.com/content/stories/local/2012/07/26/state-investigates-tutor-service.html; Holly Hacker, "Dallas ISD Alleges $500,000 in Additional Fraud by Tutoring Firms," *Dallas News*, June 2, 2012, http://www.dallasnews.com/news/education/headlines/20120602-dallas-isd-alleges-500000-in-additional-fraud-by-tutoring-firms.ece.

CHAPTER 6

1. Although the SES regulatory language clearly states that districts cannot put restrictions on instructional elements of provider programs, states have different interpretations of their own regulatory powers. For example, New Jersey put minimum qualifications on SES tutors, mandating they have teacher certification. See Frank Wolfe, "N.J. Mandates Teacher Certification for SES Tutors," *Education Daily* 194 (2011): 1–4.

2. It is important to note that while some digital vendors allowed our research team to observe tutoring sessions and speak with tutors, there were others that declined any participation in the study, and therefore we had no access to those instructional settings. The reluctance on the part of the large provider described here was minor relative to nonparticipation on the part of other providers.

Although participation in the study was completely voluntary, reluctance on the part of digital vendors to allow access to instructional settings that are paid for with public funds was frustrating for both researchers and our district partners interested in the findings.

3. RCPS developed a monitoring form for administrators and volunteers to use when doing an "Instructional Walk Through" of tutoring sessions, including digital sessions. The form had eight "look fors," or indicators of quality, such as "Rigor: Did the instruction engage students in complex, provocative, personally and intellectually challenging educational endeavors related to the mastery of standards?" or "Culturally Responsive: Did the instruction provide evidence of the teacher's awareness of students' background, cultural traditions, social experiences, prior knowledge and learning style?" Monitors checked either "yes" or "no" if the "look for" was observed and then wrote brief notes for each. The ELO office coordinated two waves of monitoring sessions throughout the tutoring season, after which the data from all forms were compiled and sent out to both schools and vendors as a point of conversation to improve learning.

4. As the district has heightened emphasis on access to tutoring by high-poverty, high-needs students, the composition and scope of participation of the steering committee widened to include the Office of ELOs as well as other departments in RCPS such as Curriculum and Instruction, Recreation, Special Education, Bilingual Education, Gifted and Talented, Professional Development, Technology, Research and Evaluation, Guidance, and Family Services, as well as representative school-level leaders, parents, and students.

5. For example, Resnick and Goodman reported that students whose families were in the lowest quartile of family income made up only 10 percent of students in gifted programs, compared to 50 percent for students from the top quartile of family income. Daniel P. Resnick and Madeline Goodman, "Growing Up Gifted" (Portland, OR: Northwest Education Laboratory Resources, 1997), 34.

6. Ernesto Bernal, "Evaluating Progress Toward Equitable Representation of Historically Underserved Groups in Gifted and Talented programs," in *Special Populations in Gifted Education: Working with Diverse Gifted Learners*, ed. Jaime A. Castellano (Boston: Allyn & Bacon, 2003); Eva Diaz, "Framing a Contemporary Context for the Education of Culturally and Linguistically Diverse Students with Gifted Potential: 1990s to the Present," in *Reaching New Horizons: Gifted and Talented Education for Culturally and Linguistically Diverse Students*, ed. Jaime A. Castellano and Eva Diaz (Boston: Allyn & Bacon, 2002).

7. Much of the literature on underrepresentation in gifted programs focuses on identification and assessment of giftedness, in many ways rooted in IQ, as the main criteria, even as it is widely assumed to be a culturally biased assessment of intelligence. Jaime A. Castellano, A. Faivus, and W. White, "Serving the Economically Disadvantaged in Gifted Education: The Palm Beach County Story," in Castellano, *Special Populations in Gifted Education*; Tarek C. Grantham,

Donna Ford, Malik Henfield, Michelle Scott, et al., *Gifted and Advanced Black Students in School* (Waco, TX: Prufrock Press, 2011).

8. Similarly, recruitment alone is insufficient, and the retention of underrepresented students is just as critical. See James Moore III, Donna Ford, and H. Richard Milner, "Recruitment is Not Enough: Retaining African American Students in Gifted Education," in Grantham et al., *Gifted and Advanced Black Students in School*, 295–322.

9. There is some indication that local policy actors are gaining leverage in education. See Julie Marsh and Priscilla Wohlstetter, "Recent Trends in Intergovernmental Relations: The Resurgence of Local Actors in Education Policy," *Educational Researcher* 42, no. 5 (2013): 276–283.

CHAPTER 7

1. Jennifer L. Hochschild and Nathan B. Scovronick, *The American Dream and the Public Schools* (New York: Oxford University Press, 2003).

2. Among others, Peter Block makes a similar point in *Community: The Structure of Belonging* (San Francisco: Berrett-Koehler, 2008).

3. Anne Larason Schneider and Helen M. Ingram, *Policy Design for Democracy* (Lawrence: University Press of Kansas, 1997).

4. Ibid.

5. These recommendations are directly informed by research conducted with Carolyn Heinrich on the implementation and effects of supplemental education services. This project is a joint effort of the Center for Health and Social Policy at the Lyndon B. Johnson School of Public Affairs, University of Texas at Austin; the Rossier School of Education at the University of Southern California; and the Wisconsin Center for Education Research and Value-Added Research Center at the University of Wisconsin–Madison. The recommendations we make are built on research supported by the Institute of Education Sciences under Goal 3 of the IES Education Policy, Finance and Systems Research Program.

APPENDIX

1. Sharon B. Merriam, *Case Study Research in Education: A Qualitative Approach* (San Francisco: Jossey-Bass, 1988), 22–29.

2. Andrea Cornwall and Rachel Jewkes, "What Is Participatory Research?" *Social Science and Medicine* 41, no. 12 (1995): 1667–1676.

ACKNOWLEDGMENTS

In qualitative research, our agenda is to understand the world of digital education from the perspective of those working inside it, and the ethics of our research approach requires that we protect the identities of all of the individuals who generously gave their time, trust, and insights into the world of digital education. This means that, regrettably, we cannot publicly and individually thank them. The individuals who helped orient us to the digital education industry and all of the subfields of that industry provided insights through interviews, sharing of white papers, conference invitations, personal blogs, podcasts, YouTube videos, and flash drives with demos and were invaluable and critical to our developing a better understanding of what was happening "upstream." We thank, too, the students, parents, teachers, administrators, tutors, and program directors who opened their classrooms, homes, databases, and minds to us and whose experiences and perspectives are reflected in chapters 2–6 in particular. We hope that we captured some of the challenges, excitement, and complexity of the work that they do and are in some small way bringing its tremendous importance into public view.

We have had the very good fortune of working with excellent graduate students on this manuscript. They pushed the work along in important ways while working long hours on their own projects and class work. These students—Rodolfo Acosta, Andrea Bingham, Christi Kirshbaum, Stacey Krueger, Wendy Marshall, Jahni Smith, Molly Stewart, and Femi Vance—were enormously generous with their time, introduced us to ideas and literatures, and provided helpful comments and contributions in all stages of the manuscript. Thanks also to our colleagues who contributed to this manuscript through dialogue and by reading drafts: Gary Anderson, Wayne Au, Stephen Ball, Regina Figueiredo-Brown, Carolyn Heinrich, Jill Koyama, and Chris Thorn, and to our editor at the Harvard Education Press, Nancy Walser.

We also thank the Institute of Education Sciences (PR/Award number: R305A090301, Education Policy, Finance, and Systems Research Program, Goal 3) for funding a portion of the research presented in this book.

ABOUT THE AUTHORS

PATRICIA BURCH is an associate professor at the Rossier School of Education at the University of Southern California in Los Angeles. Burch studies the patterns and drivers of school commercialism and the implications for the form and delivery of public education, with specific attention to equity and quality. Burch's book, *Hidden Markets: The New Education Privatization* (Routledge, 2009), examines the intersection of high-stakes accountability policies and for-profit influence on instruction.

ANNALEE G. GOOD currently serves as the research director for a mixed-method, longitudinal study of out-of-school time and digital tutoring. From the perspective of both researcher and teacher, she is dedicated to developing effective research-to-practice partnerships with school districts, specifically around access to quality digital education and extended learning opportunities. An eighth grade social studies teacher before earning her doctorate in educational policy studies from the University of Wisconsin–Madison, Good continues to teach online courses for middle school students.

INDEX

Accelerated Blended Learning Program
    (ABL)
action research project example, 70
assessment system, 85–86
assumption of quality Internet access, 81–82
centrality of the online forum to
    instruction, 78–81
challenge of going-to-scale, 87
company background, 71
compared to Computer Tutors' approach, 138
constructivist curriculum use, 70, 84, 87–88
contract specifics, 73
contrast with typical offerings to low-
    income students, 84
curriculum alignment with Common
    Core, 76–77
curriculum design, 74–76
data co-construction illustration, 181–182
data collection and use, 90–91
data system maintenance challenges, 90
engagement with stakeholders, 169–170
factors impacting low enrollment of low-
    income students, 166–169
funding sources, 73
instructional format, 77–78
instructor credentials, 88
interest in increasing access for low-
    income students, 166
open-source platform use, 71
organization of responses in the forums, 81
participant demographics, 71–72
question of what drives instruction, 183
schools' level of oversight and interaction
    with, 72
support for and requirements of teachers,
    88–89
teacher-driven instruction model results, 89

technology's importance to the learning
    process, 82–84, 89
tuition, 73
Achieve, 43
Advanced Research Projects Agency for
    Education (ARPA-ED), 14
ALEKS (Assessment and Learning in
    Knowledge Spaces), 42
American Education Researchers
    Association (AERA), 13
American Federation of Teachers, 15
American Recovery and Reinvestment Act
    (ARRA), 13
Apex Learning, 15
Apollo Group, 26
Apple, 26, 30
Arizona, 43
ARPA -ED (Advanced Research Projects
    Agency for Education), 14
ARRA (American Recovery and
    Reinvestment Act), 13
Assessment 2.0, 14
Assessment and Learning in Knowledge
    Spaces (ALEKS), 42
assessment systems
    challenge of assessing instructional
        quality in digital tutoring, 120
    Common Core's link to online assessment
        companies, 43
    considerations for vendor-driven
        assessments and data generation, 138–
        139
    instruments emerging from, 13–14, 35
    policy changes favoring investment in
        online systems, 43–45
    problems with BA's approach, 104–105, 114
    used by ABL, 85–86
    vendor control of assessments, 126–127